Turning the pages is nearly impossible when you're laughing hysterically. Refreshing and witty, *Cat Got Your Treadmill?* is the cure for what ails you. Who else but Jay would dare to compare Gene Autry with Frasier Crane?

    Pat Richley-Erickson/ *Dear Myrtle's Family History Hour*

I read *Treadmill* --- twice! It's that good. It is packed with usable, easily-comprehensible nuggets. You'll chuckle in some places, and say to yourself, "That's a great idea. Why didn't I think of that." Treat yourself and those you want to please with a copy of this book. You'll be glad you did.

    Terry Brock, speaker, marketing coach, journalist

It's rare enough to find an excellent thinker and writer. Jay Speyerer is more than that because in this book, his sharp thinking and zesty writing will help YOU do better at both! Humorous, relevant, approachable, and insightful - this is one Treadmill you'll return to again and again.

    David Newman,
    Founder of Do It! Marketing
    President, National Speakers Association/ Philadelphia

A very enjoyable read. Jay provides valuable lessons wrapped in quick wit, insightful illustrations, and poignant observations. You'll enjoy it while you learn.

    Dr. Kimberly Alyn, speaker and author,
    How to Inspire People to Achieve More

Jay Speyerer is a gifted writer whose easy-to-read style makes you feel as though you're sitting down face to face with a longtime friend. This is a must-have book for writers and speakers.

    Lisa Newburger, speaker and owner, Discuss Directives/
    Heart 2 Hearts

Also by Jay Speyerer

The Stories of Our Days
The Story System
Cat Got Your Thumb?

Cat Got Your Treadmill?

Cat Got Your Treadmill?

MORE ADVENTURES IN COMMUNICATION

by

Jay Speyerer

Legacy Road Communications
Pittsburgh, Pennsylvania

Copyright © 2011 by Legacy Road Communications, LLC

All rights reserved. No part of this book may be reproduced or transmitted in any form or by any means, electronic or mechanical, including photocopying, recording, or by any information storage and retrieval system, without permission in writing from the copyright owner.

ISBN: 978-0-9764729-4-0

Published by: Legacy Road Communications, LLC

This book was printed in the United States of America

Contents

Recognition... 13

Introduction 15

Cat Got Your Treadmill?
    UNDERSTANDING IRONY..17

Shug, Dub, and Dabbs
    WHAT'S IN A COMPANY NAME?...........................21

Pronouns: One Size Fits All?
    TINKERING WITH THE MOTHER TONGUE...............26

Signs of Intelligence
    MOST CRITTERS ARE SMART, BUT-- 30

Sounds of the Season
    SOME ARE COOL; SOME ARE JUST UNAVOIDABLE..34

Curmudgeon's Resolution: Lighten Up
    BUT KEEP PAYING ATTENTION............................39

Believe It Or Not
    RIPLEY, MOVE OVER...44

Let's Play House
    AN IRASCIBLE TV DOCTOR DIAGNOSES E-MAIL WOES....48

Writing About the Death of a Pet
    ADOPTING THE RIGHT TONE..............................53

Yancy's Dog
    RESURFACING MEMORIES....................................58

Diegesis Saves
    GENE AUTRY MEETS FRASIER CRANE 62

A Hair Piece
    NEED A TOPIC TO WRITE ABOUT?........................66

I'm Just Sayin'
    DON'T OVERTAX YOUR EXPRESSIONS......................70

Phoenix: It Was A Trip
    ACCENTS AND GRACKLES AND BUS RIDES, OH MY!........74

Speakers and the Mother Tongue
    LANGUAGE ON THE PAGE AND THE STAGE............80

The Prestige of the Story
    THE RULE OF THREES...85

Best Laid Plans
    AUDIENCES WILL SURPRISE YOU.........................88

When Jokes and Trees Fall Flat
    IF A TREE FALLS IN THE FOREST, IS IT STILL FUNNY?.....92

Media Manglings
    YOU'D THINK THEY'D KNOW BETTER.....................96

Squinting in the Moonlight
    AUDIENCE DISTRACTION IS IN THE DETAILS........100

Spectator Nation
    WE LIKE TO WATCH...104

The Times, They Have A-changed
    IS IT TOO EASY TO WATCH TELEVISION? 110

Linkbook and FacedIn
    BLURRING THE LINE BETWEEN SOCIAL AND
    BUSINESS NETWORKING 114

What It Is
    CATCHPHRASES ARE CATCHING.........................118

Merry Happy Christmidays
    A HOLIDAY GOULASH...123

Shovel-ready When You Are
    OBSOLETE WORDS AND PHRASES......................129

To Be Continued
	THOSE THREE DREADED WORDS 135

Punxutawney Philippe
	GROUNDHOG DAY ACROSS THE CULTURAL DIVIDE 139

E-mail and Antisocial Media
	YES, YOU READ THAT RIGHT 144

Brain Rot — It's Back
	OUR CHILDREN'S MINDS ARE AT RISK... AGAIN!..149

iPhone, You Phone, We All Phone
	THE THINGS I DIDN'T (AND COULDN'T) LEARN IN HIGH SCHOOL 155

for all who can appreciate a picture like this

alternative use for a salt lick no. 17

Recognition

My thanks and appreciation go out to:

Donna Herrle of Drawing Conclusions, as always, for the stylish cover design.

Kevin Cooke of Graule Studios for his patience in photographing such a finicky, demanding, and uncooperative subject. And a cat.

Melanie de Paoli for friendship above and beyond. Ask her for a cover blurb and she gives you a line edit.

Samantha Bennett for typo wrangling.

Kimberly Alyn for publishing advice.

Writers, speakers, and civilians who continually challenge me on what proper communication is.

(And, in the course of said challenges, make mistakes I can write about.)

Introduction

It's really quite simple: This book is a collection of communication articles I wrote over the past couple of years. They are presented in no particular order or arrangement, but they are roughly chronological. General topic headings are conveniently located at the top of each title page so you'll know what you're in for.

You'll find a range of subjects from irony in writing and the way music works in movies all the way to high school typing classes and why local newsreaders mangle the Mother Tongue. Oh yes, and the animals, smart and less so.

I make no claim to all the words being exactly as originally published, because I am not the same person now as I was when I wrote them. I also confess to making a few refinements in punctuation, because you can never be too nit-picky.

A few articles end with requests to my subscribers to send me their comments about the topic of said article. This applies to you, too.

Have fun.

Jay
November 2010

Writing/ Animals

Cat Got Your Treadmill?
UNDERSTANDING IRONY

Cats don't get irony, as you can plainly see in the accompanying photograph. If my cat, Fleck, did understand the concept, this tubby tabby wouldn't have chosen a piece of exercise equipment to use as a Barcalounger.

Cats get a pass on understanding the concept because they're so direct and plain-spoken. People don't have that excuse, and a lot of them don't get irony. As much as I like Alanis Morrisette, she's a bit wide of the mark with her song "Ironic" when she sings the following:

> *It's like rain on your wedding day*
> *It's a free ride when you've already paid*

The primary characteristic of irony is contradiction, either between what is said and what is reality or between what is expected and what actually happens. The occurrences in the song aren't examples of irony; the rain is just bad luck and the paid-for free ride appears to be the result of simply not paying attention. At best, they're coincidences, and irony and coincidence are not the same thing. A coincidence can be ironic, but there's no guarantee.

Both writers and speakers can put irony to good use. The writerly definition can be complex and subtly layered because irony can be couched in other literary elements. Its simplest form is theatrical irony, such as in the Greek tragedy of Oedipus, wherein Sophocles has the king all but proclaiming, "Gee, I sure hope I don't kill my father and accidentally sleep with my mother." (I'm paraphrasing the original Greek. "Gee" is a very loose translation.) This statement is ironic because he later ends up doing those very things.

This theatrical irony puts the audience in a knowledgeably superior position to the characters. The Greek audiences in the early days of theater were great aficionados of irony. In fact, they already knew the outcome of the plays they frequented since the subjects were usually something to do with the gods, whose exploits were legion. So the playwrights of the day found it easy to insert such lines as those of the aforementioned blind king.

Subtext is another tricky concept in theater and film, but it's fertile ground for irony. Say we have a detective who is looking for a bad guy, so he goes to the guy's house and interviews his mother. Mom goes on about how devoted a son Junior is. He just hasn't been around to see her because he's a busy, important man. Our detective is fully aware that Mom is not shining him on; she's in denial. She fully believes everything she's just said about her miscreant offspring. With good writing and acting, a perceptive audience will see the detective's reaction and be aware of the contradiction between the mother's words and the obvious reality.

Irony can also come in the form of sarcasm. Try saying to an overweight, out-of-shape guy who signed up to run a marathon that you're sure he'll cross the finish line right beside that epitome of sinew and bone from Nairobi. Even if he can't find the irony buried under all the snarkiness, our would-be runner will likely be offended, provided he doesn't get winded.

In Alanis' defense, there is such a thing as situational irony, wherein the outcome of an action is counter to what is expected. Example: a depressed woman wins a jabillion dollars in the lottery, but she's still depressed. However, look closely at Ms. Morrisette's example of precipitation marring one's nuptials. Why would one expect the weather gods to cooperate just for that person's special occasion? We're not talking Greek tragedy here. Such cosmic crappiness happens all the time, so if we accept that example, irony isn't really very special or difficult to achieve, is it?

Fleck has slimmed down since that picture was taken, so maybe she does get irony after all.

Writing

Shug, Dub, and Dabbs

WHAT'S IN A COMPANY NAME?

If you recognize the words in the title as the first names of great character actors from the past, you're as much of a movie and TV geek as I am.

George "Shug" Fisher was a country musician and western movie sidekick, who also appeared on such TV shows as *Petticoat Junction*, *The Beverly Hillbillies*, and *Have Gun-Will Travel*. His nickname came from his mother, who called him Sugar when he was a baby.

Better known is Dub Taylor, who played a sidekick-type character named Cannonball in a number of westerns, along with many other parts in many other movies. Dub is short for "W" which is short for Walter.

The most widely known is Dabbs Greer, who played the elder version of Tom Hanks's character in *The Green Mile*. He was also the fellow who was rescued by George Reeves's Superman in the very first episode of the series back in 1952. Robert Greer got his Dabbs moniker from his mother's maiden name.

None of those fine actors ever played a president or any other famous personage. Their names tell you why. Those were the days when the studios were reaping the benefits of the contract system, under which they pretty much took control of their actors' working lives (and sometimes their personal lives as well). That included choosing the actors' stage names. (Judy Garland was born Frances Gumm, so sometimes they were right.)

Whether the three actors chose to use the nicknames or the studio did, the choices dictated the kinds of roles they would play: sidekicks and character parts, not leads. The men themselves might have been able to play leading roles, but their names weren't.

I recall a George Carlin quotation: Attending college at a place called Bob Jones University is like putting your money in Nick & Tony's Bank. It's the same idea: the names need to match the desired image.

Imagine this remake of *The Greatest Story Ever Told*. John the Baptist will be played by Dub Taylor, Pontius Pilate by Shug Fisher, and Jesus by Dabbs Greer. There's a movie no one would pay to see. (Maybe that cast isn't so outlandish an idea after all. In the past, Jesus has been played by such non-middle eastern types as Willem Dafoe, Jeffrey Hunter, and in the actual TGSET, Max von Sydow, and he's Swedish fer Chrissake!)

Pick a name for your company and a screen name for yourself that communicate the message you want. Of course I could mention a whole raft of aptly named companies that proved to be supremely successful, such as IBM (International Business Machines), Alcoa, McDonald's, and Xerox. But that wouldn't be any fun.

There was once a company called Boring Business Systems, but the web site is no longer active, so maybe they wised up. Be careful with the screen name you choose, as well. If you're applying for a job as a kindergarten teacher, and your e-mail address is hellspawn666@aol.com, there's no way you're getting that gig. I admit to being surprised when I first saw one of the big white trucks driving around my neighborhood with "G.O.D." in giant letters on the side. Turns out G.O.D. stands for Guaranteed Overnight Delivery.

From the What Were They Thinking? Department: I pass an auto repair garage on the way to a friend's house. It's called A- Automotive. Is A minus the grade they got at auto repair school? We'll assume that the name Triple F Pet Supplies (Ontario, Canada) has nothing to do with a grade. And for years, on Pittsburgh's South Side was a diner, standing tall and proud, called Terminal Lunch.

The Internet is rife with ill-named entities. Who Represents is a site where you can find the agency that represents your favorite celebrity. Their web site address could have done with a little more deliberation: www.whorepresents.com. Experts Exchange is a kind of clearing house where you can find links to sites relating to education, finance, business, electronics, and much more. Unfortunately, they didn't put a lot of thought into the name of their web site: www.expertsexchange.com.

An online search will turn up such improbable names as the Amigone Funeral Home, Bearable Dentistry, Bender Chiropractic, the May Pop Tire Shop, and the Fractured Prune Donut Shoppe. (Their web site is a lovely shade of purple.)

Sometimes odd names work, and even a non-word will get the job done. Can you define Activia, Advanta, Integra, or Aleve? Neither can I because they're not actual words, but they have proven to work just fine as names of companies and products.

So don't decide on your company name or screen name by yourself. For something this important, you need input from people who have less direct involvement. Run it by a few friends and let them in on the fun.

Then buy them a burger at Fuddruckers.

Writing/ Language

Pronouns: One Size Fits All?
TINKERING WITH THE MOTHER TONGUE

In his article in the *Pittsburgh Post-Gazette's* "Word Watch" feature, San Diego writer Walt Meyer offers up a modest proposal for how to solve the one-size-doesn't-fit-all, masculine/feminine pronoun dilemma. I must wonder how firmly his tongue was planted in his cheek as he wrote it.

Example: A student left his or her textbook in the classroom. He or she can claim it at lost-and-found.

To replace the cumbersome he-or-she, his-or-her construction, Walt proposes new words in the form of unisex pronouns. Here's an edited excerpt from his article:

E instead of "s/he." Hir instead of "his or her." Hir would be pronounced as a homonym of hear and here. Hirs (pronounced like hears) would take the place of "his or hers." And hem would replace "him or her." (End of excerpt.)

I like the idea of unisex pronouns about as much as I like the idea of unisex bathrooms, which is not a lot. This amounts to legislation of language, and that doesn't mesh well with the natural evolution of a tongue. Our existing pronouns evolved gradually from earlier Anglo-Saxon forms. The artificial language Esperanto is an example of intelligent design, linguistically speaking, and look at how well that worked out.

One of Walt's arguments is that we "often add new words to accommodate things that simply didn't exist before." Videographer, e-mail, flight attendant, and firefighter were some of his examples.

Yes, they're new things, but the cited examples are compounds or hybrids that stem from existing and familiar root words. The solution of using such constructions as hir for him and her and e for she and he, however, necessitates fabricating what amounts to actual new words. There's the rub.

Sure, Shakespeare did it. If he needed a word that didn't exist, he made one up. But even his coinages were often variations of existing words. Of the ones he made up, some stuck around (hobnob and hoodwinked) and some didn't. Of course that was in the early stages of Modern English, before the Oxford English Dictionary was around to provide us with more than half a million choices. Besides, he was Shakespeare.

Ms. was another of the writer's examples, and I grant that it's an exception in that it's a truly new word (it's more than 30

27

years old, but that's new in the language world). *Ms.* is here to stay, but the question of whether it should be followed by a period merits a separate discussion.

Walt dislikes s/he, too, referring to it as a "sloppy construction" that he saw in a book on writing. Sloppiness be damned, I suggested using s/he in my first book, *The Stories of Our Days*, but only when writing informally. (Maybe it was my example that made his gorge buoyant. One hopes.) The first time I saw s/he in print, it was used by essayist-novelist-gadfly Harlan Ellison, but I don't know who originated it. I respectfully disagree with Walt's choice of descriptor. One person's sloppy is another person's streamlined. S/he's only shortcoming is the fact that it's unpronounceable.

I wish Walt well, and hope he has some luck in his quest. His idea would solve the problem, but it would require overt tinkering, and a living, breathing language doesn't take kindly to that.

(Make up your own mind. At the time of publication of this volume, you could still find Walt's article here: www.post-gazette.com/pg/08275/916379-294.stm)

Signs of Intelligence

MOST CRITTERS ARE SMART, BUT A FEW ARE JUST PLAIN GOOFY

Animals aren't as smart as some people give them credit for. Okay, they aren't as smart as *I* give them credit for. I used to think that most animals were relatively bright or they wouldn't have survived as a species. Collectively, they probably have the standard issue native intelligence, but there are always a few dunces who screw up the grading curve for the rest of the class. For example...

I looked out the kitchen window one day to see the bird feeder swinging crazily back and forth. I could discern movement inside, behind the Plexiglas. So I walked out to the yard to find the feeder occupied by something more than bird seed. A pine squirrel had figured out how to get into the house-shaped feeder by lifting the hinged roof panel, but it wasn't smart enough to reverse the process. They say to be careful about attributing human characteristics to animals, but I swear the squirrel had an expression of exasperated panic on its face. Staring out at me, with both paws up against the Plex, it did everything but yell "Lemme outta here!" So I did.

(Aside: One of my favorite New Yorker cartoons shows two men in suits walking by a house with a bird feeder on the front lawn. Attached to the feeder is a sign that reads "Squirrels Welcome." One of the suits sniffs disdainfully and says, "Liberals.")

Then there was the sparrow that got its head caught in the suet holder on the side of the feeder. The holder is constructed of a wide mesh of heavy-gauge wire forming a sturdy cage and is open on the top for insertion of the suet cake. Well, this bright bird got itself inside the grate work, poked its head through the grid, and then couldn't get it out. I gently put my forefinger on its forehead (do birds have foreheads?) and pushed its little cranium back through the opening, and it promptly flew away. At least it was smart enough to do that.

Plants are sprouting from the ground beneath the feeder. Some of the seeds that had been scattered by the birds and squirrels have taken root and grown. How it is that so many seeds were missed? Depending on the time of day, something is always foraging on that patch of my yard: birds, rabbits, deer, turkeys, squirrels, chipmunks, and groundhogs. Then after the day shift knocks off, the swing shift takes over: mice, raccoons, more deer and rabbits, plus the odd possum. Somehow all those critters missed all those seeds. The greenery doesn't constitute ground cover by any means, but it's significant growth. I guess it means they're not all that hungry.

Pigeons are generally recognized as not being the sharpest beaks in the coop, but I met one that qualifies as insane, if you consider the definition of insanity as doing the same thing repeatedly on the chance there will be a different outcome. By that definition, this bird was nuts.

This happened back in the 80s in the first house I ever owned. It was closer to the city and not the quiet enclave that describes my current neighborhood. (In fact, after nearly three years in this house, I have yet to see a pigeon. Is Mt. Lebanon too exclusive? Did someone put up a sign "No pigeons allowed?") Anyway, I was working in the basement and heard a muffled fluttering from the vicinity of the furnace. I finally traced the noise to the cleanout access at the base of the chimney. A bird was trapped in there.

So I opened the door and reached in and, after no little fumbling, managed to get my hands around a very sooty pigeon. It was winter, and the birds habitually sat on the rim of the chimney to get warm. The fumes probably made it woozy enough to fall in. Well, I got it out, but it promptly got away from me and flew frantically around the entire basement.

After 20 minutes or so, I finally caught it and let it out the side door. It flew up and away, making a hard right when it reached roof level. Even though I couldn't see where it landed, I knew exactly where it was headed: back to the chimney. Crazy.

The same thing happened a week or so later (five'll get you ten it was the same bird) so I did the catch and release thing all over again.

If I'd been smart, I would have put up a sign.

Sounds of the Season

SOME ARE COOL; SOME ARE JUST UNAVOIDABLE

We've talked before about the role that our senses play in memory retrieval and storytelling. In my Christmas column a couple of years ago, I suggested that you take notes about the things you noticed during the holidays. These notable things were the result of using your senses. Let's try something a little different this year. Focus on one sense: your sense of hearing.

Don't ignore your other senses; I don't want you bumping into the furniture or quaffing tainted wassail. Simply pay particular attention to what impinges on your eardrums this season, and then record them or see what memories surface. Here are some areas to note:

Music: This includes the obvious Christmas carols and seasonal hymns flooding the malls, even the ones that get stuck in your head for so long you think you'll go insane. It also embraces theme songs from TV specials and movies of the season.

For instance, hearing "White Christmas" might take you back to the first time you heard it as a kid. Or it might remind you of a couple of movies: *Holiday Inn*, where it was heard for the first time, or the later movie (also titled *White Christmas*), both starring Bing Crosby. There are worse songs to get lodged in your brain.

With me it's usually "Holly Jolly Christmas" by Burl Ives. Apologies to his fans, but both singer and song rub me the wrong way. According to humorist Dave Barry, there is actually a carol titled "Ding Dong Merrily on High." I must make a note to look that up. It couldn't be any worse.

Lines From Movies: There are almost too many classic lines from traditional holiday movies to include, but such details never stopped me before. Let's make it a quiz.

"You'll shoot your eye out."
a. A Christmas Story
b. Bad Santa
c. National Lampoon's Christmas Vacation
d. Scarface

"Zuzu's petals!"
a. A Christmas Story
b. It's A Wonderful Life
c. White Christmas
d. Scarface

"Susan, I speak French. That doesn't make me Joan of Arc."
a. Holiday Inn
b. The Bishop's Wife
c. Miracle on 34th Street
d. Scaramouche

(Answering phone) "Buddy the elf, what's your favorite color?"
a. White Christmas
b. Elf
c. Miracle on 34th Street
d. Die Hard (Hey, it takes place on Christmas)
(Answers appear at the end of the column.)

Family Expressions: Every family has them; some just aren't repeatable in polite company. Hearing them can lead to stories about how they originated. Whenever we walked into her house for a holiday gathering, Aunt Sal would say, "Park your carcass." When my Aunt Bea was just learning to talk, "snowflakes on the window sill" came out "flowsnakes on the sindywill." Ask about such sayings in your own family. Either merriment or an argument will ensue. Both are entertaining.

Accents: This all depends on your heritage and your location. If all of your family members and guests are from where you live, no one will have an accent. But if all your guests come from somewhere else, everyone will have an accent except you.

Toys: One year when I was little, Santa came through with a robot called, appropriately, Robert the Robot. He was about a foot and a half tall, with a gray plastic body and right-angled red arms that looked like I-beams. When I turned the crank in his back, I would hear a scratchy voice recite the following: "I am Robert Robot, mechanical man. Drive me and steer me wherever you can." There was indeed a control box that allowed for driving and steering, but it was connected by a stout, three-foot cable, so "wherever" wasn't very far.

Animals: I'm not referring to lowing cattle. This could be your standard dog, cat, parakeet, gerbil, or even a horse, should you have one. The sound of a current pet could lead you to stories of its latest antics (Fluffy's encounter with the Roomba) or to memories of pets no longer with us (Tweety-Bird's encounter with the Roomba).

Next to the sense of smell, the sense of hearing ranks way up there as a memory trigger. While I am very sensitive to certain smells (Holly Jolly Christmas), let's confine replies to the sense of hearing. If you can think of other sounds or anecdotes or examples, please send me a note. If I receive enough of them, I'll try for another issue before Christmas.

Merry Christmas and Happy Holidays!

You weren't really expecting the answers to the quiz, were you?

Speaking/ Writing

Curmudgeon's Resolution: Lighten Up

BUT KEEP PAYING ATTENTION

New Year's resolutions are not things I'm fond of making because their sole purpose is to program you for failure. But I have resolved *not* to do something. This year I will not go all psycho-semantic when I hear a petty, niggling example of incorrect usage of the mother tongue. (The threshold of petty and niggling will fluctuate depending on how stumped I am for something to write about.)

I've also resolved to surrender to the reality that some weirdnesses of usage will never change because the usagers don't want them to. For instance: Local television news readers eschewing auxiliary verbs in order to sound like a newspaper headline. A storm front moving in. Another witness testifying today.

Sometimes they eliminate even the main verb: A tractor-trailer accident on Route 50. I finally realized they actually like speaking that way for two reasons: it's distinctive to their profession and it ticks me off.

But there are oddities in local TV news that one simply can not ignore, such as the story about broken sewage lines that affected renters in a particular building. The news reader told us about the repair crews fixing "the ruptured tenants' lines." Apparently the tenants were trying to remove their belongings, which, apparently, were very heavy.

The preceding and following should not be construed as curmudgeonly complaints. They're simply a mélange of language oddities I've happened to notice. Onward.

Humpty Dumpty sat on a wall.
Humpty Dumpty had a great fall.
All the king's horses and all the king's men
Couldn't put Humpty together again.

Where in the nursery rhyme does it say Humpty Dumpty is an egg? (Are you finished re-reading? Welcome back.) Even if he or she were indeed a giant egg wearing clothes, and they tried to put him/her back together, how much help do you suppose they'd get from the horses?

Hold your indignant e-mails; I love horses. They're beautiful, intelligent animals, but they're not widely known for their fine motor skills. See if this scenario works for you: Dammit, I broke the handle off Grandma's antique hand-painted china teapot. BRING ME MY HORSE!

*****

When they swear you in as a witness at a trial and ask, "Do you swear to tell the truth, the whole truth, and nothing but the truth so help you God?" — what if you said no? It's phrased as a question after all, and that seems to imply that you have some options. Or are they just checking? Maybe it's another way of saying, "You swear to tell the truth, the whole truth, and nothing but the truth so help you God, right?"

They do it up right here in Pittsburgh when the court wants to communicate the weightiness of the case before it. When I served on the jury in a civil trial a few years ago, the tipstaff administered the following oath: "You do swear by Almighty God, the Searcher of all hearts, that the evidence you shall give this court in this issue now being tried shall be the truth, the whole truth, and nothing but the truth and as you shall answer to God on the last great day." That's a weighty pledge. And you'll notice that the message isn't *Do you?* It's *You do!*

*****

Has the word "classic" degenerated from meaning an example of excellence in a given medium against which subsequent efforts in that same medium are measured to simply meaning old? Go to Amazon.com and check out the "classic" TV shows available on DVD, and then get back to me.

*****

The following phrasing falls out of the mouths of TV hosts all the time when they're telling us who is going to be on the show. "Tonight we have best-selling author Jay Speyerer is with us." They start with one sentence, then shift gears and end with another. The direct object of the first construction morphs into the subject of the second. If you know the correct terminology for this phenomenon, please drop me a line. If you're one of the people committing this infraction, please stop.

*****

Good writing and speaking constitute clear communication. But sometimes the communication is not all that clear, and ambiguity creeps in. No, not ambiguity. Atrophied common sense. Be careful out there.

Uh-oh. Have I broken my resolution already?

Writing/ Speaking

Believe It Or Not

RIPLEY, MOVE OVER. WELCOME TO "SPEYERER'S BELIEVE IT OR NOT"

I once overheard an odd story in the airport in Des Moines, Iowa. This was around 1970, and I was on leave, having just completed classes at the Great Lakes Naval Training Center. Before I went home to Western Pennsylvania, I had arranged to head west instead of east and pay a visit to the family and friends of a school buddy who lived in Cedar Falls. I was catching a flight to Waterloo, which is only a couple of miles away from the small town.

My flight from O'Hare got in late and my flight to Waterloo didn't leave until the next morning. Instead of springing for a hotel room, I decided to wait at the airport and make an adventure of it by sitting up all night. I heard the story at around three in the morning, which served to elevate an already creepy tale into the realm of the truly weird.

I was traveling in my dress blues, but there were a lot of us flying in uniform in those days, so this 21-year-old kid wasn't attracting any attention slumped in my chair with my bag at my feet. I watched as two maintenance men in gray work clothes leaned on a cleaning cart and chatted in front of the small restaurant, which was closed at that time of night.

One maintenance guy was a grizzled veteran of many window washings and floor buffings, and he was telling the story to his co-worker, a rookie around my age. The older man told of something he had seen years before in that very restaurant.

He was walking behind a young mother holding the hand of her little girl as they walked into the restaurant. When the mother lifted the little girl into her chair, the man saw that the little girl had only one eye in the middle of her forehead.

His young friend was amazed. So was I. In fact, that bit of imagery kept me awake the rest of the night.

Later a few things occurred to me. As a story, it doesn't work very well except for the visual impression it makes. In fact, it's barely a story at all. There's no real structure, just a brief setup and a fast, stunning payoff. But something else also occurred to me: Was it true?

There's a concept in fiction called the unreliable narrator. For one reason or another, the person from whose point of view the story is told can't be counted on to be telling the truth, maybe because of mental illness, a hidden agenda, lack of knowledge, or general mendacity. Common examples are Henry James' *The Turn of the Screw*, Ken Kesey's *One Flew Over The Cuckoo's Nest*, and Mark Twain's *Adventures of Huckleberry Finn*.

Usually, I would regard the old guy as being unreliable simply because I didn't know him, and because the story, while possible, is fairly out there. And yet instinct makes me believe him, mainly because of the lack of detail and embellishment in his story. Shaggy dog stories tend to include too many extraneous details, but this fellow's tale was lean to the point of starvation.

I was working at a disadvantage because I didn't know either of these guys from page eight. Maybe the rookie was totally gullible and the old guy knew it and he was just shining him on, either out of boredom or to put off mopping the restrooms. But I didn't really think so because I could tell that this wasn't the first time the older man had told this story. Besides, of all the scenarios he could have made up, why that one?

One possible lesson is not to believe everything you hear. But in nonfiction storytelling, be it a family history or a business anecdote, your narrator should be regarded as being believable.

Let's Play House

AN IRASCIBLE TV DOCTOR
DIAGNOSES E-MAIL WOES

Thirty-year-old male walks into a clinic. Works in a cubicle farm, sitting in front of a computer all day. Nice guy, probably too nice. Patient presents with headache, pain in the neck and shoulders, upset stomach, and sharp, tingling pain radiating from the fingertips and up both arms, with pain being more acute in the right arm. Differential diagnosis, people.

No, his necktie isn't too tight. Come on, you know it's never the first thing you think of. Besides, that would cause fainting, not headaches. But then when he fell, he'd probably hit his head, so okay. But that doesn't explain the pain in his arms.

What? Compression of the median nerve? How do you get to carpal tunnel from a tummyache? Thank you for playing; we have some lovely parting gifts. You're fired. No, this isn't one of the easy ones. This one is more insidious. It's e-mail-related.

In the interest of curing him before he qualifies for Medicare, I'll skip to the diagnosis: the patient has CC syndrome.

The headache and pain in his neck and shoulders are the result of tension from receiving all those CC e-mails that have nothing to do with him. And yes, they can actually manifest as a pain in the neck, not farther south, as you might expect. The bellyache is from an ulcer. Hand and arm pain? That's carpal tunnel syndrome from being too conscientious in actually dealing with all these e-mails. (Okay, you're not fired after all.) Pain predominates on the right side because that's his mouse hand.

CC syndrome is epidemic, but the people who are carriers of the disease have a natural immunity. They pass along the symptoms to everyone else on their mailing list. That way they don't have to deal with the e-mail themselves. Hence, they are symptom-free.

Remember Typhoid Mary? Mary Mallon was an Irish cook living in New York City who had contracted typhoid fever as a child and still carried the bacteria as an adult. She characteristically went from the bathroom to the kitchen without stopping at a sink to wash her hands. She infected family after family around the turn of the 20th century, but didn't suffer from the disease herself.

In modern times, we no longer have Typhoid Mary; we have CC Megan. She has none of our guy's symptoms because she effectively washes her hands of the problems contained in the offending e-mail by passing along all its accompanying tensions to him.

What does CC stand for? It used to mean carbon copy, back when people used typewriters and carbon paper to make copies. But you could only make so many at one time. Too many layers of typing paper and carbon paper and the lower copies got too blurry.

When computers came along, CC came to mean courtesy copy because this nefarious practice actually used to be a good thing. Are there good CCs? Of course there are. When someone would truly benefit from knowing a decision that's been made or new information that has come to light or a change of plans.

Sadly, like many things good and true, it became corrupted. People stopped sending CCs only to those directly interested in the subject and started copying everyone in the visible spectrum, just in case someone might have even a fleeting fraction of a nanosecond's interest in the subject. And to cover their butts.

The problem is that you can send along as many CCs as you want and each one is as crisp and clear and worthless as the original. Today CC stands for caca, because 90% of these e-mails aren't worth even that. (That's from the Greek word *kakos*, meaning bad. I know you're used to Latin, but try to adapt.)

Prognosis: patient can do nothing to alleviate the symptoms except to stop investing himself in all the e-mails. But that would require a personality transplant, and that's a dangerous procedure. Besides, his insurance doesn't cover it. His only recourse: pass the offending e-mail on and infect someone else.

What's the solution? Euthanize CC Megan before she infects again.

I know, I know. I checked the doctor book and we can't do that. First, do no harm, blah, blah. The real cure rests with the senders of CCs. The prescription: Send CCs only to those with a direct interest in the topic, and to those superiors who have specifically asked to be copied on it. Take two aspirin and think before you click.

And *don't* call me in the morning.

Writing/ Animals

Writing About the Death of a Pet

ADOPTING THE RIGHT TONE

Stories about the passing of a pet have the potential of reading sloppily sentimental. You write it to purge; others read it to relate. Whether the pet is a horse or a housecat, there is certainly an audience for such pieces. This isn't one of them. Not entirely, anyway.

My friend Lulu died early in the morning of June 10, 2010. Where will I find another cat who, over the course of 21 years, played fetch; doubled as an alarm clock; guilted me into buying a bigger desk so there would be room on it for her; had such a penchant for exploring that she had to be coaxed from the roof of a house and from the crawlspace between floors of an apartment building; helped me through four moves; posed with me for a book cover; and came perilously close to experiencing the inside of a laundry chute? The answer is I'll never find another one like her, nor do I expect to.

The next cat will have his/her own quirks and foibles and superfeline abilities. For instance, my other cat, Fleck, catches moles and chipmunks — no great feat for a cat and something Lulu was never very good at — but Fleck also comes when I call her. Every damn time. If you don't call that quirky, you haven't spent much time with cats.

Other than being a tad clingy, Fleck is doing fine. With a 15-year difference in their ages, the two cats never totally bonded. A gift for my daughter Emma on her second birthday, Lulu was meant to be her Pittsburgh cat when she visited on weekends. But the cat was with me full-time since she was two months old, so the bond grew to be more like a weld. Was I devastated? Of course. Am I coping? Certainly. The question for us scribblers is how to deal with the topic in writing.

Speaking of writing, you may have noticed the relative pronoun I employed to refer to Lulu. Who, not that. The rule says who for people, that for animals and things. Sez who? My writer friend Nancy Van Iderstine once made that point, and I agree. Grammar be damned— for any being with that much personality and soul, nothing but the most personal of pronouns will do.

You've noticed by now that this piece is not akin to that emotional ambush of a movie, *Marley and Me*. If you haven't seen it by now, odds are you won't, so a spoiler alert is probably superfluous. After the audience grows attached to the frustratingly loveable mutt, the dog dies at the end, and not discretely off-screen. Oh, no. We're treated to the elderly animal being put down in graphic detail. Invoke the mantra

"It's only a movie" all you want, it's still *Old Yeller* for the new millennium.

Dead pets are the Rodney Dangerfields of bereavement. While Marley rests firmly at the sloppy end of the spectrum, occasionally you run into a sere, snarky sample from the other end. The lack of respect is evident in a recent article about Karen Litzinger's grief counseling service here in Pittsburgh, Heal From Pet Loss. A newspaper reporter presented the facts about Karen's new business correctly, but the sarcasm with which he opened the article showed detachment and a detectable lack of empathy. Phrases like "when Tippy the terrier barks his last" and "this unique, uh, undertaking" prove the point.

Full disclosure: I know Karen. She's the president-elect for my term of office as president of the Pittsburgh chapter of the National Speakers Association. Karen has as functional a sense of humor as the next person, as do I and other readers of the news article. But writing about bereavement in a sarcastic voice is a bad blend.

For those of you who are wondering about the roof and crawlspace episodes and what kind of caretaker I am, be assured. I am attentive, but Lulu was inventive. Telling such stories about your pet is probably the best way to share the good times and reconcile the loss. These stories should illustrate the unique quality of your pet or your relationship. Both at the same time if you can manage it. For instance:

Lulu was capable of creative problem-solving and of adjusting her methods to the situation at hand. (At paw?) She always woke me up early to feed her, and after trying to dissuade her, I learned it was just easier to indulge her. Since there was always food in her bowl, often my ministrations amounted to nothing more than stirring. To wake me, Lulu adopted the tactic of jumping on the dresser and using her paw to slide change off the edge, allowing the coins to clatter onto the hardwood floor.

I know this was for the express purpose of getting me out of bed because, when I moved to an apartment with wall-to-wall carpeting in the bedroom and this method no longer worked for her, she was forced to resort to the cat cliché of jumping onto the bed and touching my face with her paw. Since that apartment, all of my homes have had carpeted bedrooms. Lulu never knocked change off the dresser again.

(Since Lulu's passing, Fleck has come up with her own method of getting me out of bed: she uses her paw to try to pull down the covers.)

My dear friend Ann holds firm to the opinion that you should replace one departed pet with two. While I respect her opinion, after doing the exponential math and considering the varying possible lifespans of future felines, I determined that way lies madness and repeated visits from the health department. But I will get another pet. When it's time.

Ask me nicely and I'll tell you about the laundry chute.

Writing/ Animals

Yancy's Dog

MEMORIES CAN BE BURIED DEEP, ONLY TO SURFACE LATER

Have you ever gone to bed with a problem weighing on your mind and awakened with the answer? Popular wisdom suggests that your subconscious was working while you slept and dug up the solution. I believe the subconscious is where old memories go to hibernate.

"Traveling By Train" is a short fantasy story I wrote back in the early 90s that found a home in multiple publications. I even turned it into a screenplay. It was about a widower and his young son who return to the old family homestead for Christmas one year. The gimmick in my story was a model Lionel train that ran backwards and could take the father back in time to his childhood. In writing the story, that kind of happened to me.

As the father and son walk into the house, they're greeted by the man's elderly mother and by a friendly yellow Labrador Retriever. Petting the dog, the father exclaims in surprise, "Dixie. It can't be." Or words to that effect. The Lab looks just like the man's dog from his childhood, but the animal had been dead for years. Mom agrees that the dog looks just like his beloved childhood pet, but she assures him the dog is a recent addition to the household.

Of all my pets, I never had a dog or any other animal named Dixie. Around the time I wrote the story, my then-wife had a cat by that name, and I always assumed that's where I got the name of the yellow Lab. (Naming a dog after a cat. I know—sacrilege.) The story was cobbled up out of my nostalgia-tinged imagination, but it turns out the dog scene was likely inspired by another piece of childhood fiction.

One of my favorite shows as a kid was *Yancy Derringer*, one of the many westerns of 1958. But because it was set in New Orleans, I suppose we should call it a "southern." It starred Jock Mahoney in the title role and an actor known as X Brands, who played his mute Pawnee partner, Pahoo. A one-season wonder, the show's gimmick was the four-barreled derringer the hero kept concealed in his hat.

(Fun Fact Break: A former top stuntman, Mahoney had also played the title role in the syndicated series *The Range Rider* from '51 to '53, and he even played Tarzan in two movies in the early 60s. He was also known for being Sally Fields' stepfather. Now back to our story.)

In the single Yancy Derringer episode included in the DVD collection, Derringer goes home to the family plantation outside of New Orleans for Christmas. His late father had buried a mysterious treasure somewhere on the grounds and the location was secured in a secret place. Of course, some bad guys are after it.

Yancy enters the house and is reminiscing with the old family butler when he hears the baying of a hound outside. He says that it sounds like Dixie, but he hadn't seen the dog in seven years. He assumed he was dead.

Sure enough, Dixie is alive and well, and the Bluetick Coonhound comes bounding through the front door to greet our happy hero. An important plot point is that the location of the treasure is engraved on the metal of the dog's collar.

My ears sharpened to points when I heard the dog's name. Holy Tara, Batman! A long-lost dog named Dixie. Thought to have been dead. A happy reunion at the family home. At Christmas. In my story, the childhood Dixie makes an appearance, too, thanks to the time-traveling train. That had to be where my scene came from! The fact that Derringer's Dixie was a male coonhound and not a female Lab is irrelevant. He was a dog!

That scene had been buried in my skull for more than 35 years when I wrote the story in the early 90s. While watching the episode just last week, I could recall nothing of it from my childhood. In fact, I can remember no incident or scene from any other episode of the show either. (Maybe it wasn't such a favorite after all.)

Not having seen the show for fifty years, forgetting much of it is not surprising. But that must be where the dog scene came from. It's simply too close. To my readers who are fledgling scribblers, such things happen to writers occasionally. Not to worry, it's not theft or plagiarism or anything other than a trick of memory.

What happened to me is not that different from using something in a story that actually happened in real life, even though you might not be sure where the bit came from. The scene came to me as a result of things I either like or miss. Animals. Family. Christmas. It was the perfect answer to what I needed in the story, and my subconscious provided it.

Now if I had done such a thing consciously, it would have been borderline plagiarism, especially if I had been crass enough to not even change the dog's name. No, this scene came unbidden from the recesses of my past to fill a creative need in the present. Within my fictive arsenal, this was the ideal blend of inspiration and memory, and my subconscious pulled the trigger.

Writing/ Speaking/ Media

Diegesis Saves
GENE AUTRY MEETS FRASIER CRANE

By all accounts, the late movie cowboy Gene Autry was a fine fellow and a savvy businessman, having owned a record label, a production company, and a baseball team. He was as widely known for his westerns as he was for making a hit song out of *Rudolph, the Red-nosed Reindeer*. He made a ton of "B" westerns in the 40s, and had a TV show in the 50s, all aimed at the kid audience.

Those kids probably didn't care that Gene wasn't the greatest actor, and that he seemed to have only two facial expressions, concerned and smiling. He never knew what to do with his hands, so when he wasn't playing the guitar or punching a bad guy, he hooked his thumbs over his gunbelt. Gene's acting chops matched his voice, which was less than resonant, kind of nasal and twangy. He could carry a tune as long as it wasn't very heavy.

Sometimes Gene played his guitar as he sang for an audience visible in the movie, and that made sense in both the real and reel worlds. But sometimes we'd see Gene and his sidekick, Smiley Burnett, riding their horses along some desolate trail west of nowhere, just the two of them, when Gene would abruptly burst into song. Not only did Smiley see nothing odd about this behavior, he didn't even react to the full (and fully invisible) orchestral accompaniment that Gene seemed to carry around with him. In fact, Smiley even sang along.

Then after the song was over, the two good guys would run into some baddies. A rousing chase and fist fight would follow, with exciting music accompanying the action.

Obviously, both the audience in the story and the audience watching the movie could hear Gene's guitar when he was playing and singing for them. That's diegetic or "source" music, an actual part of the story. And just as obviously, Gene and Smiley could not hear the music when they were chasing and fighting the bad guys. That was non-diegetic music; it was there as dramatic effect for the benefit of the audience. The music Gene sang to while riding along the trail falls into a kind of music limbo.

According to Pauline Reay's book, *Music in Film: Soundtracks and Synergy*, diegesis is the story world depicted on the screen. We the audience could hear all of the music, but the characters could hear only some of it. I believe the same is true with humor.

Fast-forward fifty years. *Frasier*, starring Kelsey Grammer, was a popular spin-off of *Cheers*. Aside from being a well-written show, it was superbly cast, with each actor making us believe in his or her character. One of those splendidly fleshed out characters was Frasier's über-fussy brother, Niles, played by David Hyde Pierce.

Niles was quite the intellectual, like his brother. One day he walked into the studio of Frasier's radio program to show him a rare book he's just bought. Niles says, "I wanted to show you my copy of *Saint Katy, the Virgin*, in like-new condition." Frasier replies with a knowing grin, "Yes, well, she'd have to be, wouldn't she?" Niles smiles, and the audience laughs.

Later in that scene, they learn that their favorite restaurant is closing forever. Niles gets nostalgic for his eighth birthday party, which had been held at the restaurant, and where he was just as fussy. Niles says wistfully, "Great times. Opening presents, wearing funny hats, sending back the veal Prince Orloff." Frasier doesn't smile, but the audience laughs.

Each of those jokes is in a different form. The first one about Saint Katy is diegetic, that is, it takes place in their world and is acknowledged by the characters as being a joke. Niles smiles at Frasier's remark about the book, just as someone would do in the real world. But the other funny line would not be considered source humor. Niles' line about sending back the veal was non-diegetic. Frasier did not see it as a joke, only an example of Niles' personality.

(*Frasier* was one of the few shows I've seen where the people in the story laugh at the funny things others in the story say. Compare it to *The Bob Newhart Show*, the sitcom where he plays a psychologist. Nobody in the stories laughs.)

The second joke was character-driven; the first was not. That's the difference. We the audience could hear all the humor, but the characters could not. Just like the music in Gene Autry's movies..

Decide what kind of humor you're using in your stories, both in print and on stage. Is it a joke that other people in the story recognize as such? Or is it character driven humor that blends seamlessly with the world of the story?

If you're on stage and you tell your audience something self-deprecating and funny about yourself, it should come off as non-diegetic. You should not act as though it's funny to you; allow the audience to get it on their own. But if you tell them an actual joke - which I don't recommend unless you're a trained professional and wearing a helmet - allow the audience to know that you know it's a joke. Don't laugh at it, just acknowledge the humor.

And don't hook your thumbs over your gunbelt.

A Hair Piece

NEED A TOPIC TO WRITE ABOUT?

GET OUT AND OBSERVE

I spend a fair amount of time in Borders Café. I set up the laptop, get a cup of coffee, and work on a book project or write articles like this. It gets me away from the solitude of my office, if being accosted by two felines vying for my attention can be called solitude.

There's always someone interesting in the café, like the older gentleman who stepped up to the counter one day, scanned the coffee menu, and ordered a vanilla "late." Apparently, he was unfamiliar or uncomfortable with the foreign-sounding "latte." And the ardent young couple meeting for the first time who were textbook examples of body language that shouted "Pleased to meet you, let's trade keys." And Mr. Toupee. This fellow was mix of male vanity and selective blindness. His rug was bad. That toupee squatted on his head like a hamster on a honeydew. He wasn't so much wearing the thing as he was walking around under it.

I reasoned that Mr. Toupee either lives alone or with someone who has vision problems of their own. Because this fellow has to stand in front of the mirror every morning, don his skull-warming atrocity, turn his head side to side, and then say to himself, "Lookin' good."

Criticism is a good thing, but it's gotten a bad rap because it's taken on a negative connotation of late. Criticism at its best is simply a reasoned evaluation of what's good and what's bad about some creative endeavor. Writers and speakers are two creative types most in need of honest, unbiased, knowledgeable critiques of their work.

If you write something you're not sure works, run it by some writers who have the time and the honesty to give you a fair read. I almost wrote "writer friends," and that could work as long as you're on secure enough terms that your friend will give you an honest evaluation. A writer acquaintance is a better choice.

Back when I was teaching photography, I learned from a veteran instructor the technique of evaluating student photographs: say something nice, then cut and slice. That technique works in a lot of other situations, too.

I belonged to a writers group in the early 90s, where we met once a month and read aloud parts of what we were working on. Other members would then say what they thought of the effort. That system worked nicely until we got to know and like each other, then the cut and slice part went away because nobody wanted to hurt anybody's feelings.

Obviously you won't send off everything you write for someone else's take on it. Man up and take responsibility for the bulk of your work. But if you genuinely are unsure about a piece, ask another writer for a critique. As long as they have the time to do it for you. Actual critiques take time. Responding with a hasty "I like it" doesn't, so that could mean they're tired of providing free critiques for you.

Speakers sometimes need help, too, and there are usually two issues to deal with: content and delivery. Speakers are usually good at creating the former. Sure, maybe the order of the information could flow better. Or a story needs to be punched up. Or the closing needs work. But content is usually solid. Delivery is where the blinders take over.

Everyone has quirks in their communication style; some are interesting and endearing while others need to be toned down or eliminated entirely. I'm not referring to the tendency to fill each pause with "uh." With awareness and practice, that syndrome is relatively easy to cure.

I'm talking about hard-to-see habits such as lack of eye contact with the audience, moving without a reason, not knowing what to do with your hands, speaking too rapidly or too slowly, mispronouncing words, and letting your voice trail off at the end of a sentence. Those habits and more are better spotted by an observer or a video camera than by the speaker.

I need to re-emphasize the knowledgeable quality of your evaluators. Your family and friends who don't know the principles of writing or public speaking are not the right candidates. No matter what you do, they'll likely say something like "Very nice" or the aforementioned "I like it." Those aren't critiques, that's stroking.

So be honest with yourself and seek out valid criticism when you need it. Whether it's on the page or the stage, just like our friend with the ill-advised hairpiece, we're putting on a show. We need to be told when our toupees look bad.

Before it's too latte.

Speaking/ Writing

I'm Just Sayin'

DON'T OVERTAX YOUR EXPRESSIONS

Catchphrases float around like dandelion seeds on the wind, and every once in a while one gets lodged in your brain where it takes root and spreads until you can't ignore it any more and you finally surrender and say, "Okay, but what do you *mean*?" Such is the case with our seedling of the moment, "I'm just sayin'."

This phrase is popping up more and more lately, and to my ear, it's used to take the edge off of what might otherwise be a cutting or critical statement. "Putting on a little weight there, aren't you?." Then you raise your hands in a placating gesture, throw in a shrug, and toss off, "I'm just sayin'...."

The phrase is on a level with "all due respect" as a neutralizer of recriminations, but less refined than "not to put too fine a point on it." Jan Freeman addressed the latter in a recent installment of her language column, "The Word." It has come to mean to speak bluntly, unlike the earlier usage where the stinger was phrased with at least a hint of delicacy. Freeman says: "Writers today are much less inclined to put too fine a point on anything; the apology is now a rhetorical formula, a setup for the knockout blow."

Whereas "too fine a point" comes before the bluntness, serving as a pre-emptive strike, "I'm just sayin'..." comes after. Whatever phrase you choose, the effectiveness of these qualifiers is suspect. If you say something edgy to someone, they're immediately on their way to high dudgeon. Even if you're quick with your edge softener, they've at least reached medium dudgeon before the *I'm just sayin'* has had a chance to kick in. In other words, too little, too late.

Try it yourself. Tack it onto the end of these statements by saying *I'm just sayin'* in place of the asterisks.

That's kind of an odd color to paint your house. (***)
That's some plastic surgery they did on your nose. (***)
Wow, what a weird-looking baby. (***)

The phrase can also be used to soften an accusation. Try it again.

Joe's register was short again at closing. (***)
Ramona's bed wasn't slept in last night. (***)
Your weird uncle has been hanging around the playground a lot lately. (***)

It strikes me as being an incomplete sentence, as though the unspoken qualifier has been left off. "I'm just sayin'; I could be wrong." Or "I'm just sayin', but what do I know?" And it seems to be a requirement that you drop that final 'g' in 'saying.' Otherwise, too much weight would be attached, the casual quality would be gone, and you would have to take responsibility for the preceding statement.

That's why, when you say the phrase, you need to do your best to vocalize the ellipsis at the end. That's the three dots that signify more is to come, even though it never will. Just let your voice kind of trail off …

In the end, the phrase wouldn't even be necessary if people would do a little internal editing before they offered their opinions, or if they took the time to think about how they would feel if they were on the receiving end. So if you have something cutting to say, you should either take responsibility for your hurtfully opinionated statements or go sit on a tack.

Not to put too fine a point on it.

Writing/ Speaking

Phoenix: It Was A Trip

ACCENTS AND GRACKLES AND BUS RIDES, OH MY!

I flew out to Phoenix late last year, where I attended a three-day conference for incoming chapter presidents of the National Speakers Association. (Wait, wait— don't leave. It gets interesting, I promise.) It was a trip of many facets. In no particular order, chronological or otherwise...

It was a trip of accommodations. National must be doing well considering where we had some of our meetings and where we got to sleep. The Arizona Grand Resort is one of your posher palaces, comprising two huge villas of suites, christened Camelback and Sedona, as well as a large conference center, golf course, water park, Space Shuttle launch pad, and spa.

74

The resort is so massive that it was a little tricky finding my way around. After one late meeting in the conference center, my new friend Monica said she knew a short cut to Camelback. She did indeed know a way to get there, but "short" isn't the best descriptor. I'm pretty sure we trekked through parts of Tombstone, but she was charming company along the way, and we said good night close enough to my suite that I found it easily.

In fact, the complex was so large that at one point I fired up the laptop and used Google Earth to zoom in on an aerial view of the resort in order to find my way from my villa to that day's meeting room over the spa. Overkill? Maybe, but I got there.

It was a trip of wildlife observation. Shortly after my arrival, the clock said it was noon, but my stomach said it was two hours past lunchtime. My table was in the main section of the hotel's bright and airy restaurant, just inside the patio where about a dozen tables stood under the permanent canopy.

I was having a hamburger and coffee and admiring the view of the golf course. (I don't play, but the landscaping was pretty.) After a couple left their patio table, having finished their lunch, a grackle with the biggest feet I ever saw on a bird landed on the table and started foraging. Several other birds were checking out the other tables and the floor; apparently they were accustomed to finding food there.

The plates had been cleared and there were no crumbs left, so the grackle made do with something else. It picked up two packets of Sweet 'n Low in its beak and flew off. I mentioned this to my waitress, and she said the birds do it all the time. It seems they love any sweetener, real or artificial. The birds make a neat, surgical incision in the exact middle of the packet and devour the contents. Sugar I can understand, or even Splenda, but Sweet 'n Low?

It was a trip of accent appreciation. I love hearing different accents, and on this trip there was an abundance. We went on a field trip to NSA headquarters, which was a short chartered bus ride over to Tempe. The day we spent there was fun and informative, but it was the ride that made an impression.

Boarding the bus, I sat beside another new best friend, Rochelle, with whom I had had a nice conversation during that day's breakfast meeting. As we were waiting for the bus to leave, she took the opportunity to check in with her office on her phone. She is from the New York City chapter, and her charmingly subtle accent is pleasantly modulated and low-key. It's there, but you have to listen for it. I heard all this at breakfast, you understand. At that moment, I couldn't hear a word she was saying.

The chatter on the charter was deafening. Keep in mind these were all speakers, people who talk for a living. Well, they were talking, to new friends and old. To their seatmates. To the people across the aisle. To the driver. To a passing grackle, for all I know. All at the same time and at a decibel level that would make the floor of the New York Stock Exchange sound like evening prayers at a monastery. The person on the other end of Rochelle's call must have thought she was being held prisoner in a magpie rookery.

I had the pleasure of making a number of new acquaintances, like Justin from Columbus, Ohio. We might do a little bit of chapter collaboration during our respective tenures. Along with meeting such nice people, I had the opportunity to hear many other regional accents. Justin's is close to mine since we're both in the Mid-Atlantic (and I don't speak Pittsburghese), but other accents landed in my ear and never left.

Over the years, I've noticed that speakers from cities like Pittsburgh, New York, Philadelphia, and Boston often make an effort to tone down their accents. But our Southern friends, knowing a good thing when they hear it, crank theirs up to 11. At the end of one brief presentation by a lady who lives so far south of the Mason-Dixon Line that she can see the Equator from her house, we were all figuratively ankle-deep in corn pone and sour mash. Note: If a Southerner takes an accent reduction class, do they go through with-drawl?

It was a trip featuring a variety of fellow passengers. Thankfully, there were no security issues or annoying people to deal with en route because these topics are no fun to write about. Both the flight to Phoenix and the flight back to Pittsburgh were problem-free. My seatmates on the way to Phoenix were a young couple who slept almost all the way, barely saying a word to each other and certainly nothing to me. But the trip home was another story completely. It was The Shannon and Shawna Show.

By coincidence, Shannon works for the Art Institute of Pittsburgh, where I taught for 25 years. We played Who-Do-You-Know and Who's-Still-There. She was on the aisle and I had the window with Shawna between us, so I spent more time talking with Shawna. She was sixteen, and, sadly, going to Ohio for her grandfather's funeral. (Her mother was seated a couple of rows ahead.) After expressing my sympathies, I learned there was a lot more to this young lady.

If I closed my eyes, I could easily imagine I was talking to someone ten years older. A future teacher planning to specialize in elementary education, she lamented the lack of reading among her peers. And I learned something new, always a treat. She admitted to using her cellphone for texting, but she told me that she has friends who can text with their phones in their pockets. Touch texting, if you will. In the terminal, her mother thanked me for entertaining her daughter. I replied that she had entertained me even more.

Fascinating accents. Birds stealing sweetener. A happy, noisy bus ride. A young woman who gave me hope for the future. It was a good trip.

Speaking/ Writing

Speakers and the Mother Tongue
LANGUAGE ON THE PAGE AND THE STAGE

It wasn't long ago that I was considered too young to be a curmudgeon. Sadly, I'm growing into the role. When you think curmudgeon, the weathered visage of Andy Rooney of *60 Minutes* probably springs to mind. He can be a little cranky, though, but then again, if I had eyebrows the size and density of Yorkshire terriers, I'd be cranky, too. Until that day comes, I'll continue to make every attempt to leaven my curmudgeonry with good humor. Okay, snarky humor, but it'll be humor.

Having said that, I confess to being a bit nonplussed and unnerved — or maybe it's nonnerved and unplussed — as I witness the number of speakers who are rich in expertise, but lacking in their command of language. Language is a speaker's primary tool, the medium for our message. Artists have brushes and paints. Sculptors have clay and stone. Would you have confidence in a surgeon with a dull scalpel or a plumber who couldn't point to the business end of a plunger?

This is not true of everyone, of course. Most speakers I know have excellent vocabularies and know how to turn a phrase. (They're also no fun to write about.) However, there are enough of them who have just enough niggling little problems to hold them back and make audiences question their credentials. And that makes me want to help.

I've heard the arguments that most of the audience won't notice the errors and that as long as the message gets through, so what if there are a few mistakes. I have two answers to that: 1) Some will recognize the errors, and 2) you're supposed to be better at communicating than they are. That's one of the reasons you're allowed to be at the front of the room: because you can express yourself better than they can. The other reason is the depth of your knowledge. But knowledge isn't enough. You need the ability to clearly and confidently communicate that knowledge.

Here's the problem with a *laissez faire* attitude toward the mother tongue: Any error that people recognize, whether written or spoken, makes them stop. We don't want that. I once saw someone's status on LinkedIn that said I should use his services so I could insight my clients' needs. You can't "insight" anything because it's not a verb. And he should have known that. Did that gaffe make me stop? You bet. Did it make me question anything else he said? Double you bet.

We don't want anything to prevent our ideas from finding their way into our targets' skulls. When a reader gets to the misspelled word or the *their* that should be *there*, or the *your* that should be *you're*, or the *its* that should be *it's*, do they just ride on through? No. Not only does the pothole make them

81

stop what they're reading, but it makes them begin to wonder if what they're reading is right.

In speaking, there's good news and bad news. If you misspell a word when you're speaking, no one can tell. That's the good news. The bad news is they can hear incorrect usage and shaky grammar. For instance, here in Pittsburgh, we tend to leave out the words "to be." If something needs to be cleaned, we say it needs cleaned. To a Pittsburgher, that sounds just fine, but to anyone else, it's a pothole. (The joke goes that in Pittsburgh, Hamlet's soliloquy begins, "Or not.")

Other misuses cross geographical borders, such as saying Daylight Savings Time instead of Daylight Saving Time. The latter choice is correct. Or saying *ambiguous* when you mean *ambivalent* and vice versa. That also extends to *adverse* and *averse*, and to mispronouncing *et cetera* (hint: it's not ekcetra).

Sometimes it's not so much grammar as style. There's formal style and there's conversational style, and in writing, sometimes the choice is out of your control. I remember my first article that I ever saw in print back in the early 80s. It was an educator's newsletter called "Classroom Companion," and I was excited and surprised to have had my first article accepted.

The article was written in an early version of what has come to be my signature voice, humorously conversational. The editor kept all the humor, but s/he killed the conversational mood by eliminating every single contraction. *I'll* became *I will*. *Wouldn't* became *would not*. The content was all there, but the editing made me come off as a stuffy college professor trying to be amusing. "Harrumph. I will now be witty." Disaster.

Finally, we must be sensitive to the final use of our words. Is it the page or the stage? I was recently rewriting a preliminary script prepared by a client, preparatory to my narrating it.

One passage referred to "addressing the employees weekly via video" or some such similar phrasing. On the page, there's nothing wrong with the word "weekly," but this was to be spoken. I could be saying "weekly," but some audience members might hear "weakly." It was a small matter to change it to "every week," but you need to develop a sensitivity to such similarities.

You and I can not fix our errors unless we recognize them as such. But how can we see things we don't know are there? With a little help from our friends. We're not all sensitive to the same things, including me. I have all the fashion sense of a statue in the park, so I sometimes ask advice of friends who have been blessed with more *haute couture savoir faire* than *moi*. You might be able to point out wardrobe flaws or errors in stagecraft for someone who, in turn, can help you with language and usage issues. Make it a collaborative effort. You scratch their back, they wash your other hand.

Bottom line: It's your responsibility to be so proficient at using language that nothing gets in the way of your message. I point out problems like these for no other reason than to show off, er, I mean, help my fellow speakers. To paraphrase that famous French curmudgeon, Voltaire: I may not agree with what you say, but I'll defend to the death my right to quibble about the way you say it.

Speaking

The Prestige of the Story

THE RULE OF THREES

> *It isn't enough to make something disappear.*
> *You have to bring it back.*
> Michael Caine in *The Prestige*

I have said many times to many audiences that we as human beings dearly love the number 3. Witness the number of things that come in threes: musketeers, blind mice, stooges. (There are others, but it wouldn't be a very good example if I went beyond three, now would it?)

There are also three parts to any good illusion or magic trick. As explained in the above-mentioned movie, starring Caine, Christian Bale, and Hugh Jackman, these parts are the pledge, the turn, and the prestige. I've played around with closeup magic for years and learned in the process that a good illusion is like a good story: you can't leave off the ending.

The Prestige is a period piece, a mystery, and a love story, with a soupçon of the supernatural. Just seeing David Bowie playing Nikola Tesla surrounded by glowing arcs of electricity is worth the price of admission. The story itself deals with the rivalry between two stage magicians, as well as with the three parts of an illusion.

Let's say you want to make a coin disappear. The pledge is telling the audience that you're going to make the coin vanish. Then with a deft move, the coin vanishes. That's the turn. But the trick isn't over. Finally, you bring back the coin in a surprising way, such pulling from behind an audience member's ear or out of your nose. That's the prestige, the true payoff for your audience.

I've tried stopping with just making the coin vanish, but it always came off as unfinished. That's because I was always asked, "Where'd it go?" I can't just make up some lame joke about aliens taking it or the bad economy. The trick is unfinished until I make the coin come back. Then the audience's question becomes, "How'd you do that?"

It's supposed to be a part of the magician's code never to reveal how a trick is done. One reason is certainly about trade secrets, but it's also about economics. Once you give away the secret, the audience has no further use for you. But that's a good thing in the storytelling arena, because your audience isn't interested in writing, speaking, or presentation techniques anyway; they just want to find out what happens next and to be entertained along the way.

Be sure your stories are made up of all three requisite parts: the beginning, the middle, and the end. And be sure the proper ingredients are in each part. The pledge is the beginning, where the problem is established; the turn is the middle, where problem gets worse; and the prestige is the end, where the problem is resolved.

No shortcuts allowed. You can work magic with your stories, but if you leave anything out of the structure, your audience might be the thing that disappears.

And good luck bringing them back.

Best Laid Plans

AUDIENCES WILL SURPRISE YOU

I like to use good, vivid examples in my presentations, and I had this great idea for one about the distractions of writing. I decided to test it with a small group. (Already alarm bells should be clanging.) It didn't work very well because people are so darn helpful, bless their hearts. This was my idea:

I was off stage waiting to make my entrance while the host was introducing me to the audience of genealogists. In my left hand, I held a binder of notes and one loose piece of paper. The lectern was stage left, so I planned my entrance from stage right. That way I would have the whole width of the stage for my little maneuver.

As I crossed the stage to the welcoming applause, I purposely dropped the piece of paper, which was actually a divider, a piece of heavier stock that fell straight down to the floor without fluttering all over the place. It was in my upstage hand (away from the audience), so no one saw the deft finger move I made to "accidentally" drop it.

I knew as soon as I reached the lectern and started speaking that I had goofed.

My idea was to make a few remarks, vamping to see just how long I could draw out the suspense, and then look at the paper halfway across the stage and say, "Don't worry, I see it." Guess what the problem was with my example of a distraction. You guessed it: too distracting. (That has to qualify as irony.) The audience wasn't paying a bit of attention to what I was saying because that piece of paper bothered them.

I could have told them the cure for the common cold, how to understand the opposite sex, and how to make millions by selling second-hand cat hair. They were too busy whispering to each other.

"He dropped his paper."

"He should be more careful."

"Oh, my. He's just going to leave it there!"

One nice lady even started to climb across the apron to retrieve it for me. I told her, thanks anyway, and she returned good-naturedly to her seat.

I then crossed and stood over the paper. I said, "You know

what this is? A distraction. This is one of the things that can keep you from writing. 'I can't write,' you say, 'I have to pick up the paper.'" I eventually made my point, which they got, but it was pretty anticlimactic.

Part of the problem was the intimacy of the group. It was a small auditorium with about 50 people in attendance. I think this idea will work better in a larger venue where the audience isn't inclined to interact with the speaker.

The other problem was the fact that I was too good an actor. They believed that I didn't know I had dropped the paper. A better tactic would have been to drop the paper, get to the lectern, immediately look back at the paper and then say to them, "Don't worry, I see it." That would serve to let the audience know that it was part of the presentation and not clumsiness.

The third problem is not really a problem. Audiences are mostly pulling for the speaker. They want things to go right for you, and they get upset at a deviation from what they see as the proper way things should work. If they think you're in trouble, they worry about you.

When Jokes and Trees Fall Flat

If a tree falls in the forest and no one is there to hear it, does it make a noise? The short answer is no.

If you say something funny and no one in the room gets it, is it still funny? The short answer is yes.

Assuming the thing is actually funny, of course. Even if only one person thinks it's funny, it is. But that's not a license to be obscure. Whether you're writing or speaking, go ahead and throw in one or two just for you and the rest of the cognoscenti. But for every lofty bon mot that sails over the heads of the majority, the majority of your goodies should hit them right between the eyes. Don't be your own best audience.

The first memorable example of the subjectiveness of humor happened back when I was teaching photography at an art school. I was subbing for another instructor for two evening classes on successive days. It was an introductory class, so I introductoried myself and told them what we would be doing. Included in the intro were a few jokes and one- liners and some self- deprecating humor.

The Tuesday group was very open and receptive, laughing in all the right places. Then we got into the content of the class. It was an enjoyable evening. I did the same routine with the Wednesday group. Same intro, same humor, same flawless delivery. It was like the night of the living dead. No response. Nothing. I might as well have been speaking Finnish to Brazilians.

So sometimes it's the audience. One group will get what you're saying, whether you're spouting humor or explaining a concept, but another might not have the first clue what you're talking about. It might mean you're on a different plane than they are. But if you want to connect with your audience, you need to change planes, sometimes in midair. If they aren't responding to your humor, set it aside and go on with the information.

Humor in writing is safer. You won't know if each of your readers gets the joke or not, but at least there's no flop sweat because you don't need to time the laugh. But if you're up there speaking to a group, it's a different game entirely. Lob those high ones at your own risk. Few things are as unnerving as leaving a pause for a laugh and hearing only your heart pounding in your ears.

Speaking of ears, here's my take on the falling tree. Sound is all in the receiver of the noise, whether that receiver is the tympanic membrane of an ear or the diaphragm of a microphone. If you're near the tree when it falls, the tree's landing sets the surrounding air molecules vibrating at various frequencies. Some of those molecules vibrate against your eardrums, resulting in electrical impulses being sent along your auditory nerve to the auditory cortex of your brain, where they're recognized as the sound of a lot of heavy wood hitting the ground. Without those receiving membranes, there would just be a lot of frantically moving air molecules, but no noise.

If some people don't get your joke, let it go and move on. They wouldn't get it if a tree fell on them.

Media Manglings
YOU'D THINK THEY'D KNOW BETTER

I love the news and entertainment media in all their forms. I love anything that gives me such a wealth of material to make fun of. I mean, to point out the errors therein, thereby helping to prevent such missteps in the future. Yeah. Yeah, that's it.

Various news media have been reporting the death of William F. Buckley. The word that commentators have commandeered as the main descriptor of the man's brilliance as a writer and commentator is "erudite." Let's assume the commentators know its definition, learned and scholarly, but in the main, they seem to be ignorant of its pronunciation. For the record, the three-syllable word is pronounced *ERE-you-dite*, not *ERE-ee-you-dite*. Lose the superfluous syllable please.

One evening on ABC's half-hour news program, Chris Bury reported on the pothole problem in Chicago. Then-anchor Charles Gibson was doing the show from there, so maybe that's why they felt justified in devoting so much airtime to one city's problems with road repair.

During his report, Bury botched a Shakespearean reference. Twice. He referred to the pothole problem - which is apparently massive - as "our winter of discontent." Meaning, of course, a bad thing. Now I'm as far as you can get from a scholar of Shakespeare, but even I knew something was off. Here are the actual lines from Act I of *Richard III*:

Now is the winter of our discontent
Made glorious summer by this sun of York;
And all the clouds that low'r'd upon our house
In the deep bosom of the ocean buried.

Even when most people get the word order right, they end the quotation too soon. "Now is the winter of our discontent," they say dourly, and then stop. What Gloster was actually saying is "The winter of our discontent is made glorious summer now..."

Not only did the reporter get the line wrong, but as I learned in looking up the reference, he got the intent wrong. One: it's not "our winter of discontent," it's "the winter of our discontent..." Gloster was referring mainly to discontent, not winter. It was a metaphor. Two: things were getting better, not worse. A war was over; let the good times roll. To compound the felony, Bury ended his report by repeating the same mangled reference. The bard is spinning like a lathe.

We move beyond punctuation now to usage on the airwaves. I

speak here of the terms "theory" and "hypothesis." A theory is a set of proven facts, like the theory of gravity, the theory of relativity. If the facts are unproven, it's a hypothesis. So the next time you hear one of those talking heads on TV say, "Oh, that's just a theory," hypothesize how much fun it would be to smack him.

Let's move from national media to local. Here in my home town, Pittsburgh anchors and weather people seem to bear an intense hatred for auxiliary verbs. They say things like, "A weather system moving into the area this weekend." No "is" in a country mile. "An aide to Cyril Wecht testifying at his trial this afternoon." This goes on all the time. One of the meteorologists also manages to come up with some odd verbs to describe what the weather is doing. "A storm system buckling through the area." Buckling?

If I pounce on the media, for the sake of equal time, I must pounce on what pays their bills: commercials. This pounce is not for the language they use, which is questionable, but for the messages. Everyone has seen the commercials for various drugs that have side effects a hundred times worse than the ailments they purport to cure. That's old news, so provide your own examples. I'm talking about the one for some tricked out bottled water that has "only 25 calories." The makers claim that their water is obviously preferable to the brand containing 125 calories.

To them it's perfectly logical to ignore the fact that my tap water has no calories in it at all. Granted, it has no vitamins either, but that doesn't bother me. I get my vitamins the way Mother Nature intended: in a pill.

While we're talking about commercials, why can so few

supposedly professional announcers pronounce "jewelry" correctly? Most of the time, it comes out "joolery." And of course, gem specialists are joolers.

We can't ignore educators as sources of mispronunciation, either. I had a science teacher in junior high who pronounced caffeine as "kay-a-feen," and debris came out "der-bis." A couple years later, my high school physics teacher constantly said "irregardless." Are scientific knowledge and language skills incompatible? As I've mentioned elsewhere, I once overheard an instructor at my old place of employment, the Art Institute of Pittsburgh, tell her class that, in a job interview, correct pro*noun*ciation is very important.

Pity that all these folks weren't more erudite.

Speaking/ Media/ Writing

Squinting in the Moonlight
AUDIENCE DISTRACTION IS IN THE DETAILS

Do you squint in the moonlight because it's too bright? Neither do I. And neither does anyone else, except for the characters on TV shows from the 1950s and budget-sensitive (cheap) "B" movies. Why? Because of a cinematic technique called "day for night."

This technique was often used in those old TV shows, to which I'm addicted. The addiction is not only for the nostalgia, but as evidence that I see things in them today that I didn't notice when I was nine.

Part of my brain always wondered why the campfire wasn't brighter as Bat Masterson and his friends drank their coffee and talked about how they would catch the bad guys when the sun came up. The same section of my cerebrum wondered why the headlights of Perry Mason's car gave off so little light as he and Paul Drake arrived at a midnight crime scene. And I certainly wondered why everyone was squinting.

The reason is that it wasn't really night when the scenes were shot. It was broad daylight with the sun blazing overhead, but the cameraman underexposed the film so it would have the semblance of night. (FYI, the term "cameraman" is not sexist. In those days, all camera operators were men.)

When you underexpose film, everything is darker. Depending on what is in the shot, the technique works. But if the shot includes a light source, believability is blown out of the water because campfires and headlights are darkened along with everything else.

Shooting day for night is cheaper than paying actors and crew overtime for night shooting and going to the expense of extra lights. I'm referring here to black and white photography, where the filmmaker could put a red filter over the lens to darken the blue sky and close the lens down an f-stop. It's a bit more complicated in color. There, along with underexposure, a blue filter is used to simulate moonlight. Even though real moonlight isn't particularly blue, we perceive it as such.

"Does he have a point that relates to communication?" you ask. Why, yes, he does.

In fiction writing, we have a concept called willing suspension of disbelief. It amounts to a mutual agreement: the storyteller agrees to lie and the audience agrees to believe it. But the storyteller is still obligated not to do anything that would pull the reader/listener/viewer out of the story.

If there are mistakes in the story, the audience members' belief in the story depends whether they notice the mistakes. And that all depends on what they know. And you, the writer, don't know what they know, so you have to assume they know everything.

For instance, if you're attempting to reconstruct a conversation that took place in a bygone era, be sure the characters are using the right language. I remember an episode of M*A*S*H, one in which the actors improvised many of their lines. The story was about a newsreel film crew interviewing the personnel of the 4077th, and when they got to Radar, actor Gary Burghoff goofed.

Radar is answering a question about his mission there, and he says something to the effect that it's all about helping people and "that's where it's at." That age-of-Aquarius-era expression didn't exist at the time of the Korean War. Fiction or non, no anachronisms allowed.

No credible fiction writer wants the reader to be pulled out of the story. But if the viewer of that episode of M*A*S*H was born after the 60s, they would need an unusually sharp sense of cultural awareness to pick up on the error. But it will happen with older viewers. The seams will start to show.

In fairness to Mr. Burghoff, the responsibility didn't end with him. Either the director or the show runners should have caught the line and reshot the scene.

Maybe it's less a suspension of disbelief than it is a balance between the audience surrendering to the story and maintaining an awareness of the techniques of storytelling or filmmaking. In nonfiction, there should be only belief. The storyteller should do nothing to alter that. The writer must take great care in researching the background details.

Fiction and nonfiction are the same in that your audience must believe you and believe every word of the world you present to them. No writer wants to lose his readers. No speaker wants to lose her listeners. Pay attention to all of the details, because you have no idea whether your audience will notice the squinting in the moonlight.

Spectator Nation

WE LIKE TO WATCH

In case you haven't noticed, we're now officially a nation of spectators. But did you know we're getting worse?

Since the earliest days of television, we've been watching other people have fun winning money and cruises and household appliances on game shows such as *Wheel of Fortune* and *Jeopardy*. Make no mistake, these contestants are doing things most of the rest of us are actually able to do: fill in missing letters to make up words and phrases, and answer questions. Or in the case of *Jeopardy*, question answers.

I'm not talking about the early days of *Jeopardy* when contestants actually had to have a measurable IQ. I'm referring to the modern incarnation where many of the questions are on the level of Dick Cavett's example of a question in the California driver's test.

Should you throw glass in the street?
a. yes
b. no
c. sometimes

And then there are the televised sporting events where highly trained athletes do things 99% of us can't dream of. How many of us can hurl a javelin while swimming the Australian crawl and testing negative for Benedryl all at the same time? These shows don't count as evidence of our participatory decline (to my way of thinking, anyway, and that's what's important here) because they are examples of structured, choreographed programming involving activities most of us aren't very good at.

Today, with the advent of über-reality shows, we're in a continuing downward spiral of watching other people do things most of us are perfectly capable of doing. We must differentiate this programming from the popular reality programs like *Big Brother* and *Survivor*. These examples of being forced to spend time in close proximity to people we dislike are what we call reality TV. In real life, we call it "work."

First came the shows for people whom I call the leisure voyeurs. For instance, there are a ton of fishing shows to be found on TV. The viewer watches anglers enjoying a nice day out on the water and occasionally netting a big one. The producers of the shows are obviously hoping said viewer never gets the bright idea to turn off the TV, call his friends, fill the cooler with beer, and go fishing for real.

Then we were afforded the opportunity to watch the daily lives of celebrities, with cameras following their (almost) every move. The late Anna Nicole Smith comes to mind, as does the lamentable Lohan family. This trend began back in the early 70s with the PBS documentary of "An American Family." Members of a real family, Bill and Pat Loud and their children, allowed cameras to follow them as viewers got to watch the heartwarming story of the actual disintegration of a real marriage.

As creepily voyeuristic as that show was, programming later grew unforgivably lethargic with televised poker tournaments. Here Joe Sofaspud gets to sit around watching other people, well, sit around. Sure, the stakes are high, but the circumstances aren't exactly life threatening. There's no heavy lifting, and certainly no physical skill is required beyond refraining from shouting "huzzah" at the sight of four aces in your hand. (For the uninitiated, shouting "huzzah" is called a "tell.")

Now in the next step of TV devolution, we are offered shows where we get to watch people work. *Ice Road Truckers* is about guys driving big rigs under extreme wintry conditions, presumably without benefit of all-weather radials. *Deadliest Catch* is several steps beyond the bass fishing shows because these are real jobs that are actually dangerous.

The latest show for which I've seen promos is something called *Sandhogs*, which is either about grimy, gritty guys working in massive tunnels under life-threatening conditions or a bunch of people having a pig roast on the beach.

I haven't actually seen these shows, a fact which could be seen as invalidating my right to ridicule them. Not so; my column, my rules. But know that I have seen *Ghost Hunters*, and it's my hands-down favorite of all those other shows I haven't seen. Both American and international versions air on the Sci-Fi Channel, but the American show has the most going for it. I watch it every week.

TAPS (The American Paranormal Society) is run by two pleasant fellows named Jason Hawes and Grant Wilson. By night they head up a team of investigators who are called to various locations to investigate creepy happenings. Here they set up lots of video and audio equipment in the hope of recording some supernatural activity. The locations range from abandoned prisons to New England inns (TAPS is headquartered in Rhode Island) to private homes.

What do Jason and Grant do by day? you ask. They're plumbers for Roto-Rooter.

You read that correctly. In fact, the opening credits show their white Roto-Rooter van for a nanosecond before it morphs into the sleek black van with the TAPS decal on the side. This conceit does a great job of rooting (sorry) the guys in the real world as it shows their dedication to investigating the paranormal while sometimes showing them doing plumbing in the daylight. We never get to see what the other men and women of the team do during the day. For all I know, they're truckers and fishermen and poker players.

The show follows a rigid formula from which the guys never deviate. We see the team getting the call to investigate, then traveling to the site. During the drive, Jason and Grant get details about the location from Kris Williams, their stunningly attractive job co-ordinator. Upon arrival, Jason and Grant get a tour of the location from the owner/client, during which Jason is certain to say, "So where to next?"

Then they unload the truck and set up the gear. (This reads boring as hell, but trust me, it isn't.) Then we see the investigators through night vision and heat-sensitive cameras as they explore the darkened rooms, during which someone usually hears a noise and blurts, "What the *bleep* was that?!"

There are two investigations in each one-hour show. In earlier episodes, they got way too involved in personality conflicts between team members. They've since dropped that aspect, and the show is the better for it.

Sometimes, they get some more or less tangible results, such as ethereal if hard-to-understand voices on their audio gear and unexplained heat signatures on their thermal imaging camera. On one episode, a door opened by some unexplainable means and they caught it on camera. To their credit, sometimes the findings show absolute bupkes, which is realistic if disappointing.

After the investigation, the team evaluates the findings by going over hours of video and audio data, a task relegated to the underlings and never done by the two lead investigators. In the final five minutes of the segment, which is called the "reveal," Jason and Grant show the video and audio findings to the client and the guys pronounce the place either haunted or not.

So whether we're watching shows about truckers, fisherpersons, or moonlighting plumbers, these are not fictional stories *à la* Laverne and Shirley at the bottling plant. Let us be clear about what we're seeing when we watch these shows: we're watching real people work at real jobs for which they get paid real money under real conditions.

My question to you is this: Why is it entertaining to watch other people work? Or is it?

Bulletin: I just discovered that there's now a reality show on one of the obscure, high-numbered channels called "Parole Board." I don't even want to know.

Media

The Times, They Have A-changed
IS IT TOO EASY TO WATCH TELEVISION?

Child of the fifties that I am, I can remember a time when, if there were two different television shows I liked and they were broadcast at the same time, I had to make a decision. I picked a show to watch and waited to watch to other one during the summer reruns. Assuming of course that Mom and Dad wanted to watch the same show.

Not any more. Now I can watch anything I want whenever I want, and not just because I've achieved the age of majority. This was reinforced the other day when I realized that there are actually four decent shows running at the same time. If you're curious about my taste in television, I'm talking about Wednesday evening and choosing among *Criminal Minds* on CBS, *Lost* on ABC, *Life* on NBC, and *Lie to Me* on Fox (when it's not being pre-empted by *American Idle. Idyll.* Sorry... IDOL.) You might think I don't need to choose any more, just record them. Not so. I still have to choose.

With my current DVR (digital video recorder), I can record two shows at once, but if I'm watching that set, I have to watch one of the shows I'm recording. So I need to make a decision about which one I'm more interested in. That actually works out, because I often fall asleep and this lets me back up and see what I missed. But what about the other two shows? You guessed it: I watch them online.

Body language is one of my seminar topics, so that's why I enjoy *Lie to Me*. Besides, this is one of the procedural shows that gets the details right. I don't know about you, but it was an achievement for me to find the show on the Fox network because in the old days we had only three networks to choose from. I still have trouble thinking outside the grid of the Big Three.

Lest you think I'm a total sofa spud, know that I watch *Lie to Me* and other online shows while I'm on the exercise bike or the treadmill. Yes, exercising. We have technology to thank for this convenience, to be sure, but it comes at a price. Some kinds of entertainment aren't so special any more. We've lost a little something: anticipation.

I often wonder what Raymond Burr and Richard Boone would think about their fans being able to buy entire seasons of *Perry Mason* and *Have Gun-Will Travel* and watching them whenever they want. Many young folk will never know the joy of eager anticipation, waiting for their favorite show to come on, and the accompanying mini-sense of urgency to be in front of the set at the appointed hour. That happens less often today.

Not there on time? Not to worry. Send a command from your smartphone and TiVo it.

Movies are less special today, too, and that's because if you don't get the chance to see a movie during its theatrical run (which these days is more of a short sprint) you can always rent it or even own it. Going to The Movies used to be a special event that you even dressed up for, like going shopping downtown or taking a plane trip. Now you can watch a movie on your phone.

These media are already passive, and the marketers are making it more so by making it so easy to be entertained. Once you've mastered the simplified technology - - and we are light years beyond having to watch our VCR flash midnight because we can't figure out how to set the clock - - you need to expend very little effort to achieve your diversionary reward.

So here's my new slogan: If it's convenient, it's not special.

Media/ Technology

Linkbook and FacedIn

BLURRING THE LINE BETWEEN SOCIAL AND BUSINESS NETWORKING

Facebook and LinkedIn share some qualities with e-mail. In my *D-Mail*™ seminars, I've been telling my audiences for a long time that e-mail can be whatever we want it to be, whether we use it for business letters, casual notes, or a form of instant messaging. You can use it for all three, but confusing them can lead to disaster. The same holds true for Facebook and LinkedIn, except maybe for the disaster part. So far anyway.

LinkedIn started as the stodgy business site where you could find such announcements as "This month, I'll be speaking to the annual convention of the International Brotherhood of Flange Adjusters" and "Read my latest article in the March issue of the Wall Street Pennysaver." And on Facebook, you could find such riveting status updates as "dude hear are pics of me geting waisted on spring break sorry their out of focus" and "I'm eating cheese now."

A few changes have happened in the way some of us are using these social networking sites. Or maybe it's a change in attitude toward them. (I'm talking about these two entities because I use them. I'm on Plaxo Pulse, but I really don't pay much attention to it. And whatever happened to MySpace?)

Have you noticed a change in the respective tones of Facebook and LinkedIn? I'm seeing hints that many of us are using them interchangeably. I'm not saying that's a bad thing; I'm just throwing it out there.

Half of the issue is the get-acquainted stage of using a new site or continuing to use a redesigned one. After Facebook's recent facelift, many people are mistakenly using the status space for their replies to individual messages. They'll soon get wise. All it takes is one embarrassing faux pas.

The other half of the issue is the natural tendency to bring along our attitude toward one site when we start using a new one. Lately LinkedIn is lightening up and Facebook is forming part of our marketing strategy. And that's because of the way people are using the sites. I have many friends and contacts in both networks, and 99% of them are balanced in their use of both sites. But I've seen a few of them instigate the creeping casualness on LinkedIn and strafe us with business blasts on Facebook.

I once connected with a Facebook "friend" who was a speaker somewhere in the northern Midwest from whom I thought

I could learn something about using the site as a marketing tool. Turns out her method was to carpet bomb her friends' home pages with status updates, business announcements, and general nonsense. More than fifty per cent of my home page was a billboard for what was happening in her life alone. I had to delete all of her stuff in order to see when my other friends were picking their kids up from school and if they were out of milk. Fortunately, it's easy to hide those who wear out their welcome, and they never know it.

To get the most out of LinkedIn, join the forums and groups that are relevant to you, and then post questions or answer the questions of others. You'll get noticed in just the right way. To get the most out of Facebook, take the amateur quizzes, such as "What Flavor of Yogurt Are You?" Trust me: you'll get noticed there, too.

While a light attitude can work on Facebook, my impression is that LinkedIn users want to keep things business-like. Most LinkedInners provide us with such status updates as what job they're looking for or the fact they got a promotion. But once in a while, I'll see such notices as "I'm making toast, then it's off to work!!!!" That's not a status update, either on LinkedIn or Facebook; that's Twitter.

Don't get me wrong, I don't believe the two networks are in any imminent danger of becoming each other. But I do notice a centering trend. Contact me and let me know your observations.

If you reach me through Facebook, be sure to mention what flavor of yogurt you are.

Speaking/ Language/ Media

What It Is

The popularity of a given word or phrase is much like a hot news story. The story stays in the news until something newsier comes along to replace it. This will be a column of observations that came to me as a result of, well, observing the news.

If that seems too basic, it's probably because I've been watching too much local TV news in Pittsburgh. I watch it in the morning, but not for information. I watch to feel smart. Perhaps that's an illusion.

These reporters and news readers are, by and large, good professional communicators. But every now and then there's a hitch in their informational git-along.

These hitches often occur as they're reporting on the mandatory four topics that are required to complete any morning news broadcast in the Pittsburgh market:

Who got shot?
What burned down?
What animals were abused?
Were any Pittsburgh Steelers even peripherally involved in any of the above events in any way?

(Don't feel superior, you non-Pittsburgh markets. You have your own benighted criteria.)

During coverage of topic number two on a recent morning, a reporter doing her stand-up was explaining the nature of a business that was housed in a burning building. She began, "What it is is, the business makes insulation-" I've heard other people employ this "what it is is" construction in casual conversation (not that I have a prayer of being able to parse it), but never on a news program. This seems to be an example of verbal filler used to give the speaker a couple of extra seconds to gather his/her thoughts. But what it is is, it's verbal clutter. Onward.

In case you haven't noticed, windows are no longer "broken" according to our local newsreaders; they're "busted." When did that happen, and when will it stop?

Striving for agreement between noun and pronoun is admirable, but like anything else, it can be carried to extremes. A woman recently shot her boyfriend over a cell phone. In the reporting of the events that led to the shooting, we were treated to a description of "the couple arguing as it walked down the street."

In the Something-I've-Never-Said-And-Never-Will Department, we have this: It is what it is. This statement seems to be the new failsafe remark when you've exhausted your defenses of a position you've taken. Your conversational partner makes yet another point, but you've fired your last round and your argument ammo belt is empty. So you riposte with "Well, it is what it is." Once you've said that, you see, the person you're arguing with has to give up and stop talking. It's a rule.

And that's all I have to say on these topics. What it is is, it is what it is.

Writing

Merry Happy Christmidays

Don't you just love the smell of potpourri at Christmastime? Neither do I, but here's a potpourri/ mélange/ goulash of observations for your holiday delectation.

~ ~ ~

My friend Ann was raised Lutheran and her husband, Leon, is Jewish, so they send out Christnakkuh cards. The design is stunning in its simplicity, half stylized Christmas tree and half Star of David. By the way, the store where she buys her cards calls it Christnakkuh, so don't blame me. Probably because Chanukmas just doesn't work.

One reason this was a good year is the fact that Ann and I reconnected after not seeing each other since high school. She's the sister of my childhood best friend, Tom. When Ann or I introduce each other to a third party, the rote explanation is that we've known each other for 50 years with a 40-year gap in between.

~ ~ ~

Ann got me thinking about Christmases past, as far back as the third grade Christmas play, a rendition of "The Night Before Christmas." As evidenced by the photo at the beginning of the chapter, Dave Molter played Santa and I played his elf. Dave was a super Santa despite the wardrobe malfunction in the cuff area.

There were also a number of mice. One of the mice, Amy Lawson, still remembers her first line at the beginning of the play. She tells me that after the narrator said, "Not a creature was stirring, not even a mouse," Amy piped up, "Did you say 'not even a MOUSE?'"

I remember standing in the wings near Barbara S, who played one of the other characters. Barb wasn't sure whether it was her cue to make her entrance. I was, so when she looked at me uncertainly, I motioned her to go on. She did and all went well. In fact, the play got such rave reviews that we were held over for six months.

~ ~ ~

In your e-mails, Facebook notes, and cards to friends and family this festive season, do them a favor: use punctuation properly. (You didn't honestly think you were going to get away without a writer's rant, did you?) I bring this up not out of humbugitude, but as a public service. This is for clarity in your messages.

Apostrophes. We use this squiggle for two main purposes: contractions and possessives. If I get a *Happy Holiday's* from you, I swear I'll come over and scrooge all over your wassail. No possessive is necessary, just a plural. Send me a *Happy Holidays*, though, and I'll raise a glass in your honor for having saved a keystroke.

In a contraction, the apostrophe represents omitted letters: aren't = are not; didn't = did not; you're = you are; (for you classic poetry fans) e're = ever; o'er = over.

Commas. We all know the rule about separating the items in a series with commas, but many of us neglect another use: direct address. When we address someone by name or title, we use the comma to separate the person's name from what we say to them.

"Hello, Tom."

"Bye, all."

"Alice, please pass the turkey."

"Merry Christmas, Warden."

If you leave out the comma, your readers will get what you mean eventually, but it will take them a bit longer and you won't look as smart as you really are.

Exclamation points. There's a great website called "Overheard in the Newsroom," and one quote goes as follows: "You only get to use one exclamation point per career. Are you sure you want to use it now?" Let the words convey your excitement, not the punctuation.

Whenever I see a string of seventeen slammers at the end of a sentence, I want to knock them down like dominos. Overuse of exclamation points is annoying and distracting, but you aren't. So don't get tarred with that brush. You've known me to talk about this peccadillo before, but some of you are still committing it. If you would all simply follow my lead, life would be easier for all of us.

~ ~ ~

Slate.com has noted that the so-called "war on Christmas" has subsided this year. The media-fueled debate over "Happy Holidays" vs. "Merry Christmas" has not reached the decibel level of previous years. I have a theory about whom to thank for this: Tiger Woods. With all the related commentary, there seems to be little room for anything else inconsequential.

On a related note, here's a paraphrase of a Doonesbury quote: Unemployment expected to spike for comedy writers as 2,000 Tiger Woods jokes write themselves.

~ ~ ~

Most PC pundits will tell you that stereotypes are bad. I say they exist for a reason: so you can nod your head knowingly when you spy one and say, "See there?"

This leads me to a confession, one that I've made before in this space. I enjoy starting — and sometimes ending — my day by watching local Pittsburgh news, and not only because shaking my head in wonder keeps me limber. It's because it reflects the personality of the town I live in.

On one station, the weather guy was signing off by recapping his prediction that we would be getting one to three inches of snow. The anchor then referred to it as "an event." The weather guy paused, a bit nonplussed. (Why, I don't know. He should have been perfectly plussed considering how long he's worked here.) He then said calmly, "It's only one to three inches." The anchor then repeated, firmly, "It's an event."

That's the town in a nutshell. Many Pittsburghers like to ski, but they also like to panic and stock up on milk and toilet paper at the mere mention of snow. Case in point: I stopped at the store later for a few items (neither milk nor TP), and as I walked in, people were leaving with packages of toilet paper and gallon jugs of milk. See there?

~ ~ ~

This is the last communiqué of 2009. I hope your holidays are happy ones, however you celebrate them.

Language

Shovel-ready When You Are

The beginning of the new year is an occasion for two time-honored activities, making resolutions and breaking them. But there's a third: coming up with lists of obsolete words and phrases. Oh good, you say, something new to argue about. Well, sometimes you need to argue.

For 35 years now, the self-proclaimed "word czars" at Lake Superior State University (among others) have been publishing their annual list of words and phrases they think should be banned because of "misuse, over-use, and general uselessness." This year's compendium includes some I agree with, like "chillaxin," and some I have no problem with because I've never run across them, like "shovel-ready."

Many people dislike the latter example because it has been used in two contradictory ways: to signify that a project is ready to commence, such as a construction project, and, conversely, that a concept or project is on its last legs and is ready for the graveyard.

If it seems to you that we're living in a world of instant clichés, you're both right and wrong. Modern media have shortened the lifespan of words and phrases that would have had a longer run in days of old. And by that, I mean the 90s. But a locution lives as long as we let it. Just because some usage pundit says a phrase belongs in the scrap heap — excuse me — recycle bin, that doesn't mean we have to listen.

Present column excepted, of course. Here's one for you that I haven't seen on anyone else's list, but which is at the top of mine: Perception is reality.

I have a nicely succinct, non-profane reply to anyone who tries to get away with using that sentence in my presence: No it isn't.

Perception is perception and reality is reality, and often the twain do meet, and that's good. The problem is that the saying is never used when the way we see things matches the truth, and that's because there's no need for it then. It's the times when the disconnect seems insurmountable that many of us drag out this middle-aged saw in order to avoid the effort of coming up with an argument to refute the common lack of knowledge.

This gem is particularly infuriating because of its presumptuousness. Actually, it's presumptuous on the part of its users, along with a good dose of laziness. The term is used to bolster an erroneous opinion that is held by a large percentage of people about a given topic, implying that it must be accepted as being true simply by dint of numbers. The laziness comes from either going along with the masses or throwing up your hands and saying, "I know they're wrong, but what can I do?"

You can argue, that's what.

A recent topic to argue about is when a decade ends. Let me stop you before you say that a decade can end anywhere as long as it comprises a span of ten years. I agree. 1995 through 2004 is a decade sure enough. However, I'm sure you've seen articles and news stories touting 2009 as the end of the first decade of the new millennium.

If you're as peeved as I am about people who play fast and loose with facts, even obvious ones like when a century begins, ask them to do one simple thing: count to ten. When they start with the number one, stop them right there and say, "Thank you. I'm glad you're on my side." Then change the subject while they're still sputtering.

Sadly, logical arguments are often futile. I once dated a woman (let's call her Zelda) who was an adult student at a women's college. Walking the campus one evening, we passed a flyer for an event sponsored by a distaff organization advertising a program that had the abomination "herstory" in the title.

I had seen the usage before, but never in a serious tone. When I voiced my disagreement with said arrangement of letters (I'm trying my damnedest not to call it a word), Zelda said that history was a male view of past events and that it meant "his story." This program would be from a feminine perspective.

Zelda knew that herstory was a made-up term, but she thought it had been coined to counter an actual sexist word. I pointed out that not only does history comes from the Latin *historia* and that the ancient tongue offered no possessive pronoun called his, but that if history comes from his story, it's short a consonant. To no avail. She looked at my helpful example of etymological enlightenment the way a creationist looks at the fossil record.

I wasn't as upset at her attitude as I was at the fact that an educational institution was providing a location for a program with such a title. The program itself could have been factual and educational, but I doubt it. Yes, I judge a book by its title. My companion's perception was wrong, but it was the college's job to change her perception, not to tacitly reinforce it.

In the same vein of false etymology in the guise of feminism, I offer an item from my favorite source, local TV news. Somewhere in the Pittsburgh area recently, an elderly man slipped and fell on the ice and snow. Some conscientious and helpful young people came to his aid, comforting him until help arrived. One of the young women being interviewed downplayed their actions, claiming they weren't "heroes or sheroes."

Come now. There comes a point where we have to stop imagining that every word that coincidentally begins with a male-sounding group of letters needs a female counterpart. It will soon become preposterous.

Hebrew = Shebrew. A religious schism or a beer for the ladies?
Hedonist = shedonist. Shattering the glass ceiling of self-gratification?

Hermaphrodite = hismaphrodite. This one is giving me a headache.

If you're looking for a new year's resolution, here's one for you: keep railing at the wrongs you see perpetrated in print and in speech, or soon the whole English language will be shovel-ready.

Media

TO BE CONTINUED

It's bad enough when those dreaded words "To be continued" pop up at the end of your favorite television show, but now they're doing it in novels. You know ... books.

You can tell when the story on a TV show is going to be continued in the next episode because you're looking at your watch and it's getting close to the top of the hour and you just know they can't tie up all the loose ends in the little time that's left. But at least you only have to wait a week. Unless they pull that stunt in the season finale.

It happens in movies, too: the *Star Wars* series and the *Lord of the Rings* trilogy spring to mind. At least the audience members knew what they were in for, assuming they were willing to sit through stories told out of order (*Star Wars*), or, in the case of the Rings films, overly long ventures into fantasy. Two of the latter's installments flirt with the three-hour mark, and *The Return of the King* clocks in at a coccyx-numbing three hours and 21 minutes. And you had to wait a year to find out what happens.

I thought, naively it turns out, that books were safe. But now two of my favorite writers are doing it in their latest novel-length works. Connie Willis is an excellent science fiction author who writes with a masterful mix of humor and plotting and does some stellar things with the concept of time travel. Lee Child writes the series of unputdownable Jack Reacher mystery/ adventure novels about a former U.S. Army MP who wanders around the country righting wrongs without being weighed down by such material possessions as a car or a suitcase.

You can keep reading. I promise there will be no spoilers, unless you like the surprise of having to wait six months to find out what happens next.

This to-be-continued trend does not work for me because it violates the main rule of fiction, and it's a prime motivation for reading it: the problem is resolved. We like to read fiction because, unlike life, the problems in the story don't drag on interminably but are resolved by the time you reach the last page. The formula is so simple I feel I'm insulting your intelligence by saying it, but here goes: At the beginning of the story, a hero we can root for gets her/himself in a pickle, has a series of setbacks and escalating complications throughout, and at the end, we find out how and if s/he gets out of it. Period. End of fiction writing seminar.

In Willis' *Blackout* and Child's *61 Hours*, this rule is broken to different degrees. I was having a fine time reading *Blackout* and enjoying the multiple character arcs and timelines when I noticed with growing uneasiness how few pages remained. How can she resolve all these issues in so few pages? I soon realized she had no intention of doing so and now I have to wait until her next book is published to see what happens to everybody. Child does the same thing, but with a variation: the major story threads are tied up, but after the climactic disaster, a fairly important question is left unanswered.

I know, read a review. Well, no. I don't trust so-called reviewers not to reveal critical plot points, which the inept ones tend to do nowadays. And putting "spoiler alert" in mid-sentence halfway through the article so you have to stop reading lest you learn too much about the story is what I mean by inept. "Inept" is from the Latin for "stupid." (Not really, but I get cranky about these things.) And I'm not about to check the final pages of the book before I even buy it; I'd hate to stumble across the resolution prematurely.

Coincidentally, both continuations of the aforementioned novels are due out in October of this year, right around the time when (spoiler alert) the new TV season starts. Guess there will be a lot of cliffhangers being resolved in multiple media. Is there a way to solve this problem to everyone's satisfaction? Could be. Read my next article to find out.

Just kidding.

~Not to be continued~

Culture/ Animals

Punxutawney Philippe

GROUNDHOG DAY
ACROSS THE CULTURAL DIVIDE

Many Americans like to think our culture and customs and ways of doing things are automatically understood by the rest of the world. Not gonna happen. The next time you're feeling superior about our culture and think it's the best and most sane, you should find someone from another country and explain one of our holidays. And not one that makes sense like Thanksgiving or the Fourth of July. You should explain Groundhog Day.

On the phone.

***

Allo, Marcel? Mon ami, do you have a moment? I wanted to explain one of our holidays to you. Yes, Groundhog Day. You see, every winter, we have this celebration and tradition— Hm?

Yes, like the movie. Have you seen it?

You haven't? Well, the tradition says when the groundhog comes out of his burrow— Uh-huh?

No, it's not a pig. Groundhog Day might originate from a pagan weather festival around Candlemas and involving a badger, but that's a different animal so never mind. In America, we also call a groundhog a woodchuck. So, every winter when he comes out of his— Hm?

Woodchuck.

No, there's no wood involved. It's a big, furry rodent. Anyway, he comes out of his—

Because "Woodchuck Day" would be stupid. He comes out of his burrow at dawn in the middle of winter, and if he sees his shadow, it means there will be six more weeks of winter weather. If he doesn't see his shadow, we'll have an early spring.

Yes, "he."

Because his name is Phil, that's how I know. Anyway, it's a big celebration with lots of music and good food and— What?

How does he know to come out? Well, he doesn't. A fellow in a top hat reaches into his burrow and sort of drags him out.

Yes, as a matter of fact he has been bitten. The whole thing is a huge media event with—

No, it's not a real burrow, it's fake. He actually lives the rest of the year in the town library.

No, not the man in the top hat. The groundhog lives in the library. Look, it's a huge—

No, he doesn't live by himself. I understand he has a mate.

MRS. PHIL! HOW WOULD I KNOW WHAT HER NAME IS!? Can I finish this, please? It's a big media event with news crews and cameras and everyone just has a good time waiting to see if Phil sees his shadow. What?

Yes, the TV lights cast shadows. Look, you can make fun, but you have to admit, it must be quite an event and tradition to get people out at dawn in the middle of winter to— Hm?

February second.

Yes, I know there are six more weeks until spring anyway. Marcel, it's a nice, fun celebration and tradition. People gather a few miles outside of Punxutawney, Pennsylvania, at a little place called Gobbler's Knob, and just have a good time— What?

Punxutawney.

P-u-n— I don't know. Google it. The point is that everyone gathers around and— What?

141

Gobbler's Knob.

No, it's not what it sounds like. You know what, I'm gonna call you back and explain the Easter Bunny. *Au revoir.*

Media/ Writing

E-mail and Antisocial Media

YES, YOU READ THAT RIGHT

Are you old enough to remember those halcyon days when e-mails came only from such sources as Grandpa's steam-powered desktop computer as it chugged along the Information Superhighway? Today, we get messages from all manner of hand-held devices, many of which are dwarfed by a deck of cards. My writer friend Mary Cvetan and I were recently talking about a phenomenon that we've both been noticing for a while now: e-mails sent from iPhones, BlackBerries, and like gadgets tend to be terse and abrupt, bordering on the unfriendly.

Am I supposed to make allowances for the dinkiness of the

device? Am I supposed to ignore the snippiness and just be grateful that the sender took time from a busy schedule and deigned to flex his digits and thumb out a missive to little inconsequential me? Not gonna happen.

These notes (I can't bring myself to call them communications) also tend to be awash in misthumbings, so when you use these devices (and you will if you're not already), think for a moment about what category of communication you're dealing in. It's pretty easy to figure out because there are only two, personal and business. If it's the latter, you have no business sending the message from something small enough to get caught under your thumbnail unless you take extra special care to insure that everything — *everything* — is correct.

I've made my fair share of goofs on my iPhone simply because I wasn't wearing my glasses. Fortunately, they were notes to friends who, I hope, weren't wearing their glasses either. On the other hand, business communication has to be right every time because your reputation is on the line. (Full disclosure: I've goofed there, too.)

When you communicate in the business arena, you aren't just sending facts or information. You're putting your professional image out there in front of all and sundry. In my D-Mail seminars, to make sure my audiences know how high the stakes are, I refer to every day they send an e-mail as Judgment Day.

Communication in the business world has changed markedly over the last ten or fifteen years in that many people are now committing it themselves. These are the same folks who, years ago, would have dictated their thoughts to a secretary taking notes in shorthand. For those of you for whom disco is the Dark Ages, a secretary is a trained professional, one of whose jobs is to ensure that every piece of outgoing written communication is error-free. Today, sadly, secretaries are often called executive assistants, support staff, or this week's temp. ~~Shorthand is... Never mind what shorthand is.~~

I once heard the story of an executive who, the story teller said, was so uncomfortable with e-mail that he had his secretary print them out. He then made notes on them for his reply, after which he gave them back to his secretary, who typed them and sent them off to e-mail land. It later occurred to me that maybe the guy wasn't uncomfortable with the medium; maybe he just knew his assistant was better at spelling and grammar than he was. If so, kudos to him.

We've dealt with the so-called social media in these pages before, but I need to elaborate. E-mail can indeed be social if the writer treats it like a letter. By that I mean taking the time to craft proper sentences using just the right words to convey subtleties of meaning and emotion. It's called composition.

(I'm lumping e-mail and Facebook together in this instance because so many people's styles are the same no matter which medium they're using. If you're not thinking of e-mail as a communication medium, start.)

Sorry, but I still have a problem calling Facebook a social medium. There's nothing social about sitting at your computer in your jammies at 2:00 on a Sunday afternoon and updating your Facebook status when you haven't even brushed your teeth yet. If it's anything, it's dangerously anti-social. Whoever came up with the social media moniker was either having fun with irony or they were communicating in "newspeak" *à la* George Orwell's *1984*. (I refer you to the Ministry of Truth.)

The term is frustratingly slippery. They hand you sociability in the first word and then take it away with the second. If an experience is mediated, it isn't social. A medium is a conduit for information, sure, but it's also a separator of sender and receiver, a barrier to using all of your senses and experiencing an event first-hand.

Are media the Devil's work? Of course not. Media are valuable and necessary channels for communication and entertainment. TV is a medium, snail mail and e-mail are media, Facebook is a medium. The first is asocial (no chance of face-to face); the second and third are social, but at a remove (face-to-face not immediately possible perhaps); Facebook is anti-social (used to make comments to people you'll probably never have the chance to meet face-to-face or would even want to).

Lately, Facebook has been co-opted by business people as a way of keeping their names in front of potential or current business associates. Never mind that LinkedIn is a better tool for that; we'll talk about that another day. If you use Facebook in this way, you need to pay attention; even there, the essential concepts of business communication apply. Spelling, grammar, usage — the whole nine yards.

Because we can now employ our mobile devices to create not only e-mails, but Facebook status updates and messages as well, the possibilities of miscommunications are greater than ever. The more conduits we have, the more careful we have to be.

Put your glasses on and proofread.

Media/Culture

Brain Rot — It's Back
OUR CHILDREN'S MINDS ARE AT RISK... AGAIN!

Warning! Keep your children away from this insidious communication medium. It will turn them into lazy, pudding-brained slugs, fire up their libidos to uncontrollable levels, invade your privacy, and set our entire society on a course to intellectual collapse. I'm speaking of course about books. And about telephones. And silent films. (Those new talkies? Don't worry about them; they're just a passing fad.) Oh, and paperback novels. And television. And cartoons. And comic books. And computers. And the Internet. And instant messages. And cell phones. And texting.

Why is every new mode of communication always suspect? This suspicion, of course, always comes right after the latest medium has been trumpeted as being the greatest idea to come along since pockets on shirts.

And why do the suspecters always say the peril is aimed at our kids? Because these naysayers are not as young as they once were, and older people are suspicious old poops with chronic neophobia (fear of anything new) and young people are angelic sprites with open and inquiring minds (neophilia?). (Note to self: Never generalize.) (And use fewer parentheses.) There's also the fact that kids automatically gravitate to whatever hot new item their parents detest, and the elders, in turn, sneer at whatever the young folks latch on to. And that, Grasshopper, is called the circle of life.

The Greek philosopher Socrates is actually on record as coming out against the idea of the written word, saying that it would cause a lapse in critical thinking because a student would not have to exercise his memory, thus causing it to atrophy. Another reason he had for disliking books — scrolls, actually — was because you couldn't have a dialogue with one. No matter how many times you read it, the damn thing just kept saying the same things over and over. Said "record" comes from later philosophers, such as Plato, because no writings by Socrates exist for the simple fact that he didn't like to— well, you know.

Socrates might have been on the right track about memory, at least numerically. In this age of speed-dialing, how many of us actually remember individual phone numbers anymore? We can now carry around our personal phone directories in our BlackBerries and iPhones and such. But fear not; worries about this "new laziness" are overblown. Didn't the little address books that we used to carry around (and some of us still do) accomplish the same thing? You still had to use your little book to look up all those numbers you didn't call regularly. Besides, not needing to remember phone numbers these days frees our minds for other things. Like remembering where we left our phones.

Telephones are such a big part of our lives that it's quaint to consider that in its early days it was regarded solely as a means of business-to-business communication. After all, one fellow argued, who in their right mind would want one of those noisy, invasive contraptions in their home? Times and attitudes do change. Now we carry them around in our pockets and watch movies on them.

You've probably heard of the Catholic Legion of Decency and the Hays Office and their list of things that couldn't be depicted in the movies. This was back in the 1930s, when filmmakers had such draconian restrictions as: no showing the inside of a woman's thigh, no police as bad guys, and not even a hint of sex outside of marriage. They weren't too crazy about sex inside of wedlock, either. This lasted until 1967 when director Arthur Penn pulled out all the stops with *Bonnie and Clyde*. This opened the door to the era of movie-making where nothing is left to the imagination. Cool. Now we don't need to exercise that anymore either.

Restrictions such as these, however, lasted much longer in the world of television. One that lasted for years dictated that the good guy could never fire his gun first. He always had to fire in self-defense. I can recall a number of times when this rule made the hero look as though he had the reflexes of a snowman. Then we got through the seventies to the eighties when the rules and story lines on broadcast television started to loosen up a little. Then cable came along and more stops were pulled out and a new generation of brains were in danger of putrefaction. (And this was before *Jersey Shore*.)

Television did not limit its intellectual carnage to the young folk. Writer Harlan Ellison has told of older ladies who would dress up in the privacy of their homes to watch their favorite soap operas. The reason they donned their Sunday best?

Because their friends were coming to visit. Yes, they thought the TV actors could see them.

There's a quote floating around from an early adopter of computers who opined that there would never be a need for a computer in the home. Lacking foresight, he was correct only at the time, considering he probably said this just after the era when a computer was a collection of vacuum tubes and switches housed in a container the size of your average tractor-trailer.

This comment still made sense later when the standard electronic brain had been engineered all the way down to a box no bigger than an Amana side-by-side refrigerator/freezer. Back then, computers were only good for none-to-swift numerical calculations and not for playing Fantasy Football during working hours. I like to imagine this fellow was a descendant of the man who couldn't envision a telephone outside of a business office.

The only medium on my arbitrary list that could have used some control in the early 50s were comic books. I'm not talking about Superman battling Lex Luthor or Archie asking both Betty and Veronica to the prom. I'm referring to "comics" that depicted murder and mayhem and graphically bloody beheadings — on the covers, no less — and then being sold to tots. And so the Comics Code Authority came to be, watery and tepid as it was. Now after years of calm in the comics world, we're in the age of the "graphic novel." Blood is back.

I won't go into cell phones and texting because you've heard it all before, and recently, I'll wager. I'll just fall back to my original theme: the reason kids text so much is because adults don't like it. So when you youngsters all get GPS chips embedded under your tattoos so all your friends will know where you are and what you're doing every waking and sleeping minute, the curmudgeons will inveigh against that, too.

The point of all this, as you may have gathered, is that no matter what the new brain-killing medium might be, we survive it. Kids still grow up and go to college and get good grades and good jobs. The horror stories you hear in the news media are the exceptions. That's why they're news.

We always survive. That's one reason you won't hear any grousing from me. Another reason is because I'm so hip. I text often. I've also been exposed to all of the aforementioned media and my gray matter still functions well enough to write about them in this space and speak in front of audiences. Coherently, so far.

But I have to go now. Don't want to miss dessert. Brain pudding tonight!

Technology

iPhone, You Phone, We All Phone

THE THINGS I DIDN'T
(AND COULDN'T)
LEARN IN HIGH SCHOOL

Think back to your high school years. Did you take a typing class? I wish I had.

I'm talking about typewriters here, not computers. My generation had no such gadgets in high school. Nothing electronic, anyway, beyond transistor radios. We didn't even have digital calculators; we had slide rules.

For those of you whose birthdays fall after that of Texas Instruments, a slide rule is a calculating device that looks like a thick ruler. A narrow strip covered with numbers slides in a precisely fitted groove within a larger strip, also festooned with digits. It's one evolutionary step above an abacus, but with a lot of training and practice, it can be used for such tasks as propping up the short leg of your kitchen table.

At least the typewriters at my school were electric, but I never learned how to use one. If I could retrieve all the time I've lost by retyping something I screwed up because I wasn't looking at the screen, I could make several pots of coffee. Needing to re-type passages has a deleterious effect on my ability to communicate in writing because of the disruption in the flow of my highly nuanced, delicately phrased prose.

No, seriously.

What's the problem? you ask. Just learn to type. Or as some would say these days, learn to keyboard. (FYI, I refuse to recognize keyboard as a verb. When you drive, you don't car. When you cook, you don't stove.)

At my high school, for reasons known only to the powers that were, typing wasn't offered to those of us in the academic program, but rather only to students in the business program. Presumably, we academics would one day hire the business grads to do our typing for us.

Oh, I've tried to learn to type by using the program "Mavis Beacon Teaches Typing." While I found it useful and even fun, I reached a point where Mavis got too tough on me. I was doing fine with the home keys and such, because the graphics of the program offered a keyboard on the screen. There I could see ghost versions of my fingers on the virtual keyboard as I typed.

That feature was a useful cheat because I was effectively looking at the keyboard. I was progressing nicely, learning where all the keys were and getting accustomed to using the majority of my fingers. But eventually, as I progressed through the levels, I stalled. This was because I was required to pass time trials in order to advance. I couldn't do that, so I quit. Besides, I rationalized, if I'm practicing my typing, I'm not writing.

Now comes the crowning insult. Did you know there are blank keyboards on the market? Blank as in no markings at all on any of the keys. To this non-touch typist, people who use this kind of keyboard to write, transcribe, or enter data are doing those things only secondarily. Mainly they're just showing off. (This article is cross-filed under "sour grapes.")

If you want to see a picture of one of these Devil-spawned keyboards, just Google "blank keyboard." As you'll see in the picture, these keyboards are sleek and black and cool and shiny, and I'm totally intimidated. (You won't see that last part in the picture, but you can imagine.) Really now, what other possible purpose can blank keyboards serve other than to allow the hyper-proficient keyboardists to lord it over the rest of us?

If I had to categorize the blank keyboard, I'd have to call it useful, but showy. Same goes for the *i*Phone. Yes, I have an iPhone. I admit right off that it screams self- indulgence. Look how I can take pictures, look how I can send text messages, look how I can send e- mails. Why do you think they call it an **i** Phone? (Don't let that unassuming lower-case *i* fool you; it's all about ego.) I have to admit that I do like the phone, now that I'm accustomed to its peculiarities. I find it much easier to take care of problems now that I've learned treat it like a computer that has telephone capabilities, rather than as a telephone that lets me get online to see if it's going to rain.

157

For instance, sometimes the thing can't check my e-mail because it can't find the network. Instead of assuming the network is down, I simply shut off the phone, wait several seconds, and then turn it back on. That's the same way I solve problems with my desktop or laptop computer: shut it down and reboot.

No slide rules these days, thank you. Modern high school students have a Radio Shack inventory of electronic devices in their backpacks, such as calculators, game players, cell phones, and music players. Now, of course, these are more than likely all combined in one device. But if any of them lose their battery chargers, they're toast.

So yes, I have succumbed to the siren song of the *i*Phone. But even if I could type, would I buy a blank keyboard? You bet your abacus.

Jay Speyerer is a former educator and professional photographer, a current writer and speaker, and a future past-president of the Pittsburgh chapter of the National Speakers Association. He lives in Pittsburgh and makes no apologies for it.